The SOCCER MOM MYTH

Today's Female Consumer:
Who She *Really* Is,
Why She *Really* Buys

Michele Miller & Holly Buchanan

Wizard Academy Press

Austin, TX

Printed in Canada

Wizard Academy Press

16221 Crystal Hills Drive
Austin, TX 78737
512.295.5700 voice, 512.295.5701 fax
www.WizardAcademyPress.com

Ordering Information

To order additional copies, contact your local bookstore, visit www.WizardAcademyPress.com, or call 1.800.425.4769
Quantity discounts are available.

SC ISBN: 978-1-932226-79-9
HC ISBN: 978-1-932226-56-0

Library of Congress Control Number: 2007932941

First Printing: March 2010

For Ron, who has always encouraged me
to fly high enough to touch the moon.

—Michele

To Buck Buchanan,
"the last honest man in advertising"

—Holly

CONTENTS

ACKNOWLEDGEMENTS

Sir Isaac Newton once said, "If I have seen farther than others, it is because I have stood on the shoulders of giants." We are deeply indebted to the philosophy and teachings of Roy H. Williams, and Jeffrey and Bryan Eisenberg of Future Now Inc., which have provided the rock-solid foundation of the book you have in your hands.

Roy H. Williams has long been a researcher in the field of brain wiring, human behavior, and language. Without his wealth of knowledge and awe-inspiring perspective, this book might never have happened. To learn more about the wide variety of classes offered by Roy and an impressive list of faculty, visit www.wizardacademy.com.

A large portion of this book is focused on marketing to women online. We discuss the techniques of uncovery, creating personas and planning scenarios, which are all part of Future Now Inc.'s methodology known as Persuasion Architecture™. We also discuss the four buying modes used in Persuasion Architecture™. To learn more about Persuasion Architecture™ or Future Now Inc., visit www.futurenowinc.com.

Michele's Personal Acknowledgements:

I never understood the author who thanks their significant other at the *end* of the acknowledgements, often saying something like, "Last but not least, I want to thank my husband/wife for all they've done, for their great sacrifice and support." What's with the "last but not least" business? If they're so great, why not thank them *first*? So, here we go: To my husband, Ron, for showing me a level of support I never knew existed, for the freedom to let my beagle roam wherever it wishes, and the empathy that can only come from another creative type. You are my inspiration to fly.

I thank Roy H. Williams and Pennie Williams, the dynamic forces behind the Wizard of Ads enterprise and Wizard Academy. Their support, encouragement, and butt-kicking (only when necessary) opens new worlds each and everyday. I am honored to spin in their orbit and to call them business partners and friends.

Thanks to Corrine Taylor, Sean Taylor, and the rest of the staff at Wizard of Ads, Wizard Academy, and Wizard Academy Press. To my partners in the Wizard of Ads firm, thank you for the knowledge, support, and laughter you shared with me during this writing project. Thanks to Jeffrey Eisenberg, for the numerous phone conversations that always ended with my brain clicking at a level I hadn't thought possible.

Last, but not least (sorry, I couldn't help myself), I send a heart full of thanks to my co-author Holly Buchanan. What started out as a small project blossomed into a book of which we're both quite proud, and the blessing has been working with someone who balances my working style, thought process, and sense of humor. Holly, you are a joy (even if you do make fun of how I dance).

Holly's Personal Acknowledgements:

I thank Bryan and Jeffrey Eisenberg for giving me the opportunity of a lifetime, the chance to work at Future Now Inc., a company that proves you can be highly successful but still have a soul.

To my friends and family: Lee Buchanan, Maggie Hyrkas, Bog Gobright, Boris, Natasha, my Richmond posse, my NY posse, and to my sister, Heather Buchanan, a special thanks for letting me borrow some of your best lines. Writing and researching this book kept me from attending more dinners, dog walks, sunsets, golf games, late night gab fests, and just plain quality time with you all, yet you've remained steadfast in your support. Thank you. Many of you also offered your opinions, insights and personal stories. (Ok—maybe *offered* is too strong a word, but hey, I'm a writer, if you tell me something, there's a good chance it will end up in print. Get over it.) This is a far better book because of your input.

To all the uber smart folks Future Now Inc.: Howard Kaplan, Anthony Garcia, Melissa Burdon, John Quarto-von Tivadar, Jeff Sexton, James Maher, Robert Gorell, Lisa Davis, Marijayne Bushey, Esther Eisenberg, Bill Schloth, and all you other fabulous folks.

The biggest thank you of all goes to Michele Miller. Pretty much the whole reason I took on this project was to get a chance to work with such a talented, insightful, funny whackadoodle. You rock. I can't wait to conquer the world together.

PART I

How to Market to Women

1

The Soccer Mom Myth:

Why Women Aren't Responding

The room was a marketer's dream filled with educated, savvy women with money and the urge to spend it. Our *Marketing to Women* seminars attract professional women who, in their rather *spare* spare time, are also enthusiastic shoppers.

We hadn't launched into our dance routine yet (long sordid story for later), so we still enjoyed some respect from the audience. Holly asked a pointed question: "How many of you in the room consider yourself a Soccer Mom?" The silence reached a crescendo and nary a hand rose.

At most of our seminars, about 60 percent of the audience are women. Yet every time Holly asks that question, usually only one or two women raise their hands. So, Holly qualifies by saying, "How many of you are moms?" Usually a great many hands go into the air.

Now, we're not so bold as to ask actual ages, but by eyeballing the crowd, it's obvious that the vast majority of these moms fall into the twenty-five to forty-five-year-old Soccer Mom range. (Yes, there could be some older women who don't look their age. You know what they say: fifty is the new forty, forty is the new thirty.)

But even taking that into account, the numbers never change. Usually only 1 to 2 percent of the crowd identifies themselves as a Soccer Mom. If you listen to marketers and politicians, there are millions upon millions of Soccer Moms out there, yet in our seminars we've found only about *seven.*

What's going on here? Why aren't more women identifying themselves as Soccer Moms? Come on, there's nothing wrong with being a Soccer Mom, right? *Right?*

If women don't consider themselves Soccer Moms, what does that say about the effectiveness (or *ineffectiveness*) of billions of dollars of advertising aimed at this group?

Women Aren't Responding

Seventy percent of all women say marketing doesn't speak to them. Twenty years ago, even ten years ago, this wouldn't have been surprising. But now? Advertisers have finally woken up and realized women are responsible for 80 percent of all purchasing decisions. They're making a concerted effort to reach out to this "niche." They're conducting specialized research; they're creating specialized "women-focused" marketing teams; they're doing their best to try to speak to and understand this audience.

So why the disconnect? Why are so many of their efforts failing? Some people point to advertising creatives and corporate executives and say, "Because men are making the decisions. Men don't understand women." We have one word for that, *horse hooey.* (OK, it was two words.) You can't blame it all on men. Women are responsible as well. Yes, there are still more men than women in decision-making positions in companies, marketing departments, and advertising agencies. But women hold such positions, too, in ever-increasing numbers. They are a part of the decision-making process.

The truth is, both women and men have biases, and both believe in many of the same stereotypes. Both women and men are gathering all sorts of marketing data and coming to the same flawed conclusions. We're not here to place blame, but we are here to point a finger. That finger is pointed at the customer, because at the end of the day, all the answers lie with her. She's the one we're focusing our attention on.

Frequently Asked Questions

When we tell someone we specialize in marketing to women, the words are barely out of our mouths before the listener starts blurting out questions. We've gathered together some of the most pressing questions we get from business owners and marketers and used them as the basis for writing this book.

You're probably asking some of these questions yourself:

- *What do women really want?*
- *What can you say to them to get them to buy your product or service?*
- *How can you get inside their heads to find out what their true motivations are?*
- *How can you create and market products that are remarkable?*
- *How can you create messages that not only get their attention but also get them to act?*
- *Do women process advertising messages differently than men do?*
- *How do you market to women without turning off men?*
- *If stereotyping helps you better understand your audience (Soccer Mom is a stereotype) why is it so harmful to your marketing efforts?*
- *What are the factors you need to take into consideration to make sure you generate a positive response, and that women associate that response with your brand?*
- *Which marketing mediums are most effective for reaching women? Are you better off sticking with traditional marketing mediums (television, radio, print)?*
- *Men are traditionally the early adopters of new technology. Since women are supposedly not technically savvy, should you even be considering more high-tech mediums like the Internet, blogs, podcasting, etc.? Which marketing mediums consistently deliver the highest return on investment (ROI)?*
- *Should a man or a woman create your marketing campaign? Should a man or a woman design your website?*
- *How do you transfer your offline marketing skills to your online marketing strategy? How can you take the success of traditional media—radio, print, television, etc.—and apply it to your website?*

- *How do men and women use the Internet differently?*
- *When designing websites for women, should you use softer, pastel colors, pleasing wallpaper backgrounds, and give them lots of choices for browsing? Or will that actually work against you?*
- *What are women's biggest pet peeves when it comes to advertising?*
- *When should you create a "women only" area? Should you have separate areas of your website devoted to women? Should you create products for women only? Or is it best to work the features and benefits women want into your existing website or product?*
- *How do you handle a woman's objections? Is it best to address her possible objections about what you're trying to sell to her? Or is it better not to plant a negative thought she may not have even been thinking about and instead stay focused on the positive benefits of your product or service?*

We've spent years working with marketers and companies of all sizes, from small businesses to large organizations like Best Buy, Timberland, Lincoln Center for the Performing Arts, Leo Schachter Diamonds, Acceller, GE Healthcare, HP, and Volvo International. We've tackled all of these questions and many more, and have come up with solutions based on hands-on experience.

Forget *Why*—What We Want to Know Is *How*

Today's rallying cry is no longer "Why market to women?" It's "*How* do we market to women?" That's what you'll learn in this book. The secret lies in going beyond stereotypes and finding ways to truly understand who women are and what they want. Because here's the thing: *Not all women are the same.*

OK, we hear the "duhs" reverberating around the room. But then why do so many marketers lump all women into one category? Why do they believe all women act, think, and buy the same way? Why do they say, "We understand Soccer Moms," and then think they can speak to every mother between the ages of twenty-five and forty-five the same way?

Yes, there are certain biological factors, traits, and communication styles that many women share. We'll talk about some of these common principles and how to use them to increase the effectiveness of your marketing.

But that's just the beginning. The real value of this book is in creating **personas**; understanding the different segments of your audience, different personality types, buying preferences, and information-gathering techniques. You'll learn how to identify and relate to the different types of women you want as your customers. Note that we'll be referring to Persuasion Architecture™ personas as discussed in Bryan and Jeffrey Eisenberg's book, *Waiting For Your Cat To Bark*.

You see, women aren't a niche. In terms of almost every product category, they are the majority of purchasers, even categories traditionally dominated by men. In addition to the traditional female categories of spending, women are responsible for more than 50 percent of all do-it-yourself purchases, 51 percent of consumer electronics, 89 percent of bank accounts, and 80 percent of healthcare.

The other true value of this book is our strong focus on one of the most exciting opportunities for reaching women: *Marketing to women online*. Their time spent with traditional advertising mediums is declining, while their time spent on the Internet is increasing. For many reasons, the Internet is the perfect advertising medium for reaching women. Many websites either fail in their attempts to persuade women or don't make any attempt at all. There is a *huge* opportunity here.

To take advantage of this opportunity, you must understand some fundamental differences between men and women, how to identify what the different segments of your audience are, and how to create relevant messages that truly resonate with your female audience on an individual level.

Marketing to a Woman: The New Mainstream

She's 51 percent of the population and controls 80 percent of all purchasing decisions. She is not a fad or a niche. Rather, she is, in many cases, the majority of your audience. Several factors have converged to make her a more powerful purchasing force than ever.

Understanding Gender Differences: Nature Versus Nurture

Don't make the mistake of marketing to women the same way you market to men.

Men and women are different; no surprise to any married couple, but a wake-up call for marketers. Biological and societal differences create a real difference between the sexes. Women have different buying methods than men do, they have different priorities and look for different information, and they have different interests and expectations.

Understanding those differences is critical in order to take advantage of each gender's natural preferences.

The Power of Marketing to Women as Individuals

Are you addressing all women the same way? Your message may be resonating with some but not with others; in fact, it might even be alienating them. Women are very different from one another. You cannot judge a woman by demographics alone. Even the subgroup of mothers includes a huge variety of psychographics. You have to recognize women as individuals.

One of the biggest reasons marketing fails is because advertisers are marketing to stereotypes. You must have a deeper understanding of who she is and how she operates. It is all too easy to fall into the stereotype trap. How do you avoid that trap? How do you gain that deeper understanding? One word: *Personas.*

The basis for creating personas is good uncovery. But be careful. What research methods are you using to gather information on your customers? Many companies have tons of data on their customers. They do a lot of quantitative research, but they don't always do a good job of interpreting that data and turning it into quality insight. More attention needs to be paid to *how* you gather the information, *what* information you gather, and what you do with it. Here's a hint: Focus groups and traditional studies may not be giving you the information you really need.

Taking that into account, personas will give you the deeper understanding you need to talk to your audience and address their different needs, motivations, and buying methods. You'll learn some of the basics of how to create personas and, more importantly, create persuasive scenarios where both your customers and your business can achieve your goals.

Uncovery and personas are both part of the Persuasion Architecture™ methodology developed by Future Now Inc.

Marketing to Women in the New Digital Age

In the good old days of advertising, if you wanted to promote a product, you bought television, radio, print ads and billboards, or sent out direct mail. Now the media choices are almost unlimited. New technology is putting more control than ever into the hands of the consumer. She can tune you out more easily than you think. The good news is, there are new channels that are a perfect fit for women. If you want them to hear your message, you have to know which channels hold the most opportunity for highest return on investment. Plus, you need to understand the importance of delivering a consistent message in today's multi-channel advertising environment.

Will Marketing to Women Alienate Men?

There are all sorts of opportunities to speak to, do business with, and gain the loyalty of female customers. But here's the best part: Companies have found that their efforts to satisfy their women customers have had a surprising side effect: Their male customers are more satisfied as well.

How can that be? Keep reading, and we'll show you how.

2

Victory Lady Fitness:

A Success Story

In 1989, Wendy Messner opened a small fitness club for women only in Richmond, Virginia. She started from scratch with zero members. Today, Victory Lady Fitness has two locations of fourteen thousand square feet and more than thirteen thousand members.

How did Wendy Messner take a start-up and turn it into a multimillion-dollar success story?

Wendy doesn't have a business degree, but she has business smarts. She won't work with anyone who doesn't respect her, she's very demanding and savvy, and she's incredibly independent. But we believe the true secret to her achievement is due to two things. One, she's passionate about what she does. Two, she understands her customers. Wendy knows women. Many times, she's disregarded "expert" advice and has succeeded because she *didn't* listen.

In the following chapters, we'll talk about the things you must do if you want to understand, reach out and relate to your female customers in a way that's meaningful to them and very profitable for you. Wendy has used almost every technique; perhaps intuitively, but it's worked.

So, how does she do it?

No Stereotypes

Victory Lady isn't chasing after buff young women (the stereotypical core of fitness club members). Wendy talks to deconditioned women, many of whom never even dreamed of setting foot inside a fitness club.

One of the club's most popular longtime instructors is Shirley, a large African-American woman who is, we'll just say, quite a ways past her twenties. Shirley may do more talking than moving, but we guarantee when you finish your workout, you'll feel like a million bucks.

Nothing is typical at Victory Lady Fitness. The clubs don't feature traditional female colors or decorating styles. There are no pastels or pinks.

Victory Lady offers a staggering number of cardio machines, but *every* member is assigned a weight-lifting routine, including free weights. Every woman is trained in using weights to build strength.

You won't find run-of-the-mill yoga classes at Victory Lady. Wendy and her team design all the classes, combining a variety of techniques. Their most popular class is kickboxing.

Bold Club Colors—Red and Black

Walk in the door of Victory Lady Fitness, and you're immersed in a world of red and black. The entire back wall is painted red. Is this really a fitness club for women? Experts would suggest Wendy "soften" her colors to some nice pastels, pinks, or yellows, colors that are more traditionally "feminine." But Wendy instinctively knew red and black were the right colors for the message she wanted to convey; she wanted to energize and empower her members.

When you look up the meaning of these colors, here's what you'll find. In the philosophy of yoga and meditation, red is associated with the first chakra, muladhara (root support). It is a hot color that represents life energy, physical strength, and vitality. Red is a very emotionally intense color. It enhances human metabolism, increases respiration rate, and raises blood pressure.

Black is equated with the night universe, lack of falsehood, divine energy; the absence of color. Black gemstones symbolize self-control and resilience. Black stones have protective energies. Key words used to describe black include banishing, protection, absorption and destruction of negative energy, independence, strength, fascination, allure.

Remember, Wendy's message is energizing and empowering women. Think she could have picked two more perfect colors?

High Energy Radio Spots With a Male Announcer

Radio ad reps suggested Wendy use a female announcer on her commercials, with nice jazzy music in the background. Wendy didn't listen. She wanted a strong male announcer and hard-rockin' music, because she feels women listen more to men. Wendy wanted prospective customers coming through the door pumped up with high energy. If they walked in with a more energetic, positive state of mind, she had a better chance of them joining the club.

Real-Women Marketing Before Dove and Nike

For her television spots, Wendy makes sure the videographers film "ordinary" women. She doesn't just photograph fit, young women in hundred-dollar aerobic outfits; she makes sure her commercials feature those actual club members who are deconditioned. Many wear oversized T-shirts, not midriff-baring sports bras. They are real members with plus-size bodies. Wendy does this on purpose—deconditioned women are her market. She wants women to see themselves in the ads. She wants them to know they will fit right in at her clubs. Wendy was featuring real women in ads long before Dove and Nike launched their famous campaigns.

No Doors on the Front Area Offices

These offices are where salespeople take prospective customers to talk to them about joining. When you close a door in this situation, women can get nervous. They feel trapped. They wonder what you're going to say that you don't want the rest of the club to hear. By not having any doors, there is a feeling of openness and transparency. Victory Lady has nothing to hide. Hard sell and hype have no place in the sales process.

Understanding Her Whole World

When talking to prospective members, Victory Lady employees find out about these women's lives as a whole, from family to jobs. They get to know them in a complete context so that they can better understand the customers' deeper motivations and needs. Quite often, a member's real reason for joining isn't as much about fitness as it is about a deeper motivation or goal.

It's Not About Price

If a prospective customer doesn't join, no matter how many times she says the problem is price, it isn't. There's usually another objection that hasn't been addressed. Victory Lady employees make every effort to get to the bottom of each and every objection.

Never, Ever, *Ever* Talk Down to or Belittle Your Customers

Wendy and her staff are trained to relate but never to be condescending to their members. They do not judge. They do not suggest a woman should join to lose weight unless she specifically states that as her goal. Questions are welcomed. There are always staff members ready to show a member how to use machines or equipment. The whole goal is to reduce intimidation.

Build Relationships

Despite being the owner and having a thousand demands on her plate, Wendy still teaches classes. She doesn't sit behind a desk in an off-site office.

She's in the clubs every day, out on the floor, talking to the members. How often do you have daily contact with a CEO? How many CEOs would still teach classes?

Creating a Sense of Belonging

Wendy knows an amazing number of her members by name. She has party days, offering special classes and cash giveaways. She maintains strong ties with older members (some have been with her all seventeen years since she opened) and includes them in welcoming new members.

Victory Lady's image is a prized asset. Wendy does not sell logo merchandise. The only way you can get a Victory Lady hat, T-shirt, or workout bag is by being a member. You have to join and then reach a goal, or win something in a contest or event. Every member of this club is made to feel special and a part of the Victory Lady community.

Word-of-mouth Marketing

Wendy does a huge amount of "bring a friend" marketing. She encourages all members to talk to their friends and offers specials where both the member and her friend get a special rate. Free printable guest passes are always available on the Victory Lady website so members can bring friends to try the club for free. On party days, she encourages members to bring nonmember friends to join in the activities.

Ask For and Use Customer Feedback

Wendy was considering making her clubs "no cell phone" zones. But before she made a unilateral decision, she asked for feedback from her members. Boy, did she get it! One side refused to be without their cell phones. It was their lifeline to a child at home or to work, and the only way they could be contacted in an emergency. Others were sick of the distraction caused by loud yakking from neighboring treadmill walkers. Her members were equally split. So Wendy posted all the feedback, then made the decision to allow cell phones if members talked quietly and kept chatter to a minimum. By including the members in the decision, she empowered her members and reduced complaints, because they had a chance to voice their opinions, and more importantly, their opinions were heard.

Be an Expert

Wendy and a local television station created the "Victory Minute," sixty-second vignettes where Wendy gives exercise tips and advice. Wendy has spent her entire adult life in the fitness industry and shares her knowledge freely with the audience. She is known throughout the city as the expert in women's fitness.

Contributions to Charities That Share Her Passion

Wendy supports local organizations by donating fitness equipment. She donates to a variety of organizations, from fire stations to schools. She doesn't do it for the recognition; she does it because she believes in the benefits of getting strong and fit and gaining the self-esteem it can offer. Her charitable contributions are directly tied to her personal passion.

In Tune with Trends in Technology and Marketing

Victorylady.com is a key strategy for building and maintaining relationships with members. Wendy partners with other women-friendly businesses in the area to offer specials to her members on the website. Visitors can sign up for the *Victory Lady Newsletter,* which promotes events at the club. Anyone can go to the website and download a free one-week pass. There's a personal video message from Wendy. Members can also download the latest class schedules. Wendy does *not* sell her e-mail list to third parties. It's probably worth a fortune, because it's any advertiser's dream to have access to active, affluent women. But Wendy values her members' trust and privacy.

Victory Lady is the success it is today because of the marketing savvy of Wendy Messner. Wendy's achievement is remarkable because *she's built a business that's remarkable.* She isn't trying to be all things to all people. She focused on a hole in the fitness-club market (the narrow niche of deconditioned women) and did everything she could think of to speak to the needs of those customers.

Victory Lady also has something no other club in town has: Wendy herself. Because of her personal presence and passion, not only did she build the brand; she *is* the brand. No one else can duplicate that.

While you may not be able to clone Wendy Messner, you, too, can experience this kind of success. What it takes is a deeper knowledge of what women really need. All you have to do is put that knowledge into practice.

Passion + Knowledge x Practice = Success in Marketing to Women.

We're here to give you the knowledge you're looking for; the rest is up to you.

Are you poised for victory?

PART II

Marketing to Women: The New Mainstream

The New Mainstream

It was the timidity and fear of magazine editors that served as the catalyst for a book that changed the world forever for American women.

In the late 1950s *McCall's*, the most popular women's magazine of the time, commissioned one of its regular freelancers to write a story about the "life of the happy housewife" in post-World War II America. When the young writer Betty Friedan came back to the editors with an essay on the increasing restlessness of American housewives, her article was met with skepticism and even some hostility. American women, Friedan wrote, were not happy in their narrow roles as housewife and mother and were quietly talking among themselves about this "problem that had no name."

McCall's rejected the article, then *Redbook*. Then the editors at *Ladies' Home Journal* rewrote it to state the exact opposite of Friedan's point. Pulling the article before it could be published, a distraught Friedan called her agent from a New York subway station. "I told her, 'I'll have to write a book to get this into print.' What I was writing threatened the very foundation of the women's magazine world—the feminine mystique."

Three days a week, Betty took the bus from Rockland County into New York City, where she diligently worked on the book from a quiet corner in the Allen Room of the New York Public Library.

The book took five years to complete.

The rest, as they say, is history. Betty Friedan's treatise, *The Feminine Mystique,* rocked American society and was the catalyst for what has been called the "Second Wave" of feminism, the call for equal rights in education and the workplace. Editors, writers, and critics were outraged; American women were inspired and empowered. The message of *The Feminine Mystique* became the rallying cry of women across the country and spawned the women's liberation movement led by Friedan and Gloria Steinem.

Since its publication in 1963, *The Feminine Mystique* has sold more than three million copies, has been translated into numerous languages, and is considered one of the best nonfiction books of all time. Betty Friedan wrote a new introduction for each decade of reissue (to accompany the original introduction). These offer a fascinating aerial view of her perspective on the metamorphosis of American women (better yet, all of American society) since the book's original publication.

Betty Friedan died on her eighty-fifth birthday. We'd like to think she went peacefully, knowing her life had purpose and had changed the world. We'd also like to believe she was watching over the latest transition of American women with delight, an era where women are rallying for equality in media, advertising, and marketing. Without Betty Friedan, who knows how much longer it would have taken us to get to the crest of the Third Wave.

> *Grown-up men and women . . . become more and more authentically themselves. And they do not pretend that men are from Mars or women are from Venus. They even share each other's interests, talk a common shorthand of work, love, play, kids, politics. We may now begin to glimpse the new human possibilities when women and men are finally free to be themselves, know each other for who they really are, and define the terms and measures of success, failure, joy, triumph, power, and the common good, together.*
>
> — Betty Friedan
>
> Introduction to the 35th Anniversary Edition of *The Feminine Mystique*, 1997

3

The Third Wave:

The Real-Life Challenge of Marketing to Women

Marketing to women doesn't work. Companies of all sizes have jumped on the marketing to women bandwagon over the last few years, eager to take advantage of a demographic that possesses superheroic purchasing power. They've absorbed a glut of statistics stating that at least eighty cents of every consumer dollar in the United States is either directly spent or influenced by women. They've launched marketing to women campaigns, initiatives, projects, strategies, and battle plans. And with the exception of a few specific triumphs, they've failed miserably.

This marketing to women thing is a bunch of baloney, they say. *We reach out to women consumers, we're "female-friendly," and we're still not getting very far. Nothing we're doing makes any difference when it comes to the bottom line. Marketing to women? It's a complete waste of time.*

Interestingly enough, they're right.

At least, when you view it from that perspective. Somewhere in recent years, these marketing executives and business owners read or heard that "marketing to women" was the next field of dreams. They believed that by simply "connecting" with women, acknowledging their purchasing power and changing the look of their advertising, they'd be on the high road to the promised land of astonishing profit. Imagine their surprise, then, when this "build it and they will come" strategy didn't produce the expected results.

It's true that in the twenty-first century, women wield enormous purchasing power. A hefty wad of money has been sitting prettily in the palm of the female hand for some time now. So then why is marketing to women only *now* emerging as a hot topic? Why aren't more companies successful in their marketing to women efforts? Is it really, as they say, just another "gimmick"?

Hardly. What at first glance may appear to be a random marketing fad is, in fact, deeply rooted in the recent past and is here to stay. The answers to the questions "*Why now*" and *"What do we need to do to succeed?"* lie in history *and* provide us with a vision of the future. Before you can determine how you will succeed in marketing to women, you first need to understand why female consumers are indeed the market of the future.

How We Got Here

In a way, you could say the era of marketing to women arrived by way of a "perfect storm," an analogy that refers to the legendary 1991 storm off the East Coast, later made famous by Hollywood. A perfect storm is born when several smaller forces converge at an optimal moment, producing a massive powerhouse that's nearly indestructible.

While some may see the marketing to women era as a random occurrence, we actually see it as the third in a series of important eras or "waves" that have changed the lives of American women and the perspective of society as a whole during the last one hundred years.

In our research, we've found something interesting. If we review the last century, we see that historic milestones for American women occurred thanks to the confluence of *three critical elements:*

- the role of women in society at a given time.
- the banding together of women in a concerted effort to make their voices heard.
- the emergence of a new form of communication technology.

In 1920, women gained the right to vote for the first time after declaring their intention to fight for equal rights. It hadn't been easy; it had taken fifty-four years of marching, protesting, and imprisonment to finally triumph. So what was the tipping point for this *First Wave* of feminism? Communication to the masses through the power of the press and by means of the newest invention in the home, *the telephone.*

From the 1920s to the 1940s, women discovered the world was theirs for the taking. They were enrolling in college in droves, focusing on careers in science, medicine, law, and the arts. Magazines of the time, including *Ladies' Home Journal*, published articles on politics and world affairs by award-winning journalist Walter Lippmann, and fiction by the noted writer William Faulkner. In these stories, women were portrayed as brave souls with the world at their feet; they were explorers, adventurers, even bush pilots. This feeling of freedom compelled American women to step up to the plate during World War II and fill the jobs of warehouse supervisors, shipbuilders, and airplane mechanics while their men were overseas.

Immediately after World War II, society and advertising threw women a curveball. Almost overnight, Rosie the Riveter morphed into Hannah the Housewife. Ads for toothpaste and kitchen appliances offered the "solution to catching a husband" and beauty cream was promoted with the question, "Does Your Husband Look Younger Than You?" In the 1950s, a computer manufacturer advertised its new product with a photograph of a smiling housewife in her kitchen and the headline, IF SHE CAN ONLY COOK AS WELL AS HONEYWELL CAN COMPUTE.

Enough is enough, said Betty Friedan, who sent tremors throughout society in 1963 with *The Feminine Mystique*, a scathing analysis of the role of women in 1960s America. Suddenly, the country was experiencing a *Second Wave* of feminism. The call that demanded equal opportunity in education and jobs spread like wildfire, thanks to images of female protestors and bra burners that flickered on nightly TV newscasts.

Advertisers, too, began to pay attention and spent the next several decades creating marketing and products "made for a woman," often dripping with feminine virtue and tied with a pink bow. Virginia Slims was right in 1969 when it joined the ranks of women's lib and proclaimed, "You've come a long way, baby."

But there was still plenty of room for improvement.

Marketing to Women: A Third Wave Rebellion

Jump ahead another forty years to the current day. A *Third Wave* rebellion is under way, and not just against the pervasiveness of male-based messages in advertising. Today's woman is swinging her purchasing power around like David's slingshot, aimed directly at the Goliath of traditional advertising and marketing.

Gender equality is not necessarily the issue anymore. What women are calling for now is recognition in the form of *consumer parity.* She wants to be acknowledged as an *individual consumer with individual needs,* rather than as an anonymous member of the female demographic.

In society today, women are reaching higher planes of self-awareness at earlier ages, and along with that self-awareness is the growing desire to connect with products and services that resonate with the inner self. "I know I'm a woman," she's saying. "But I'm not like *every other* woman. Would you please start speaking to me about *what matters to me?*"

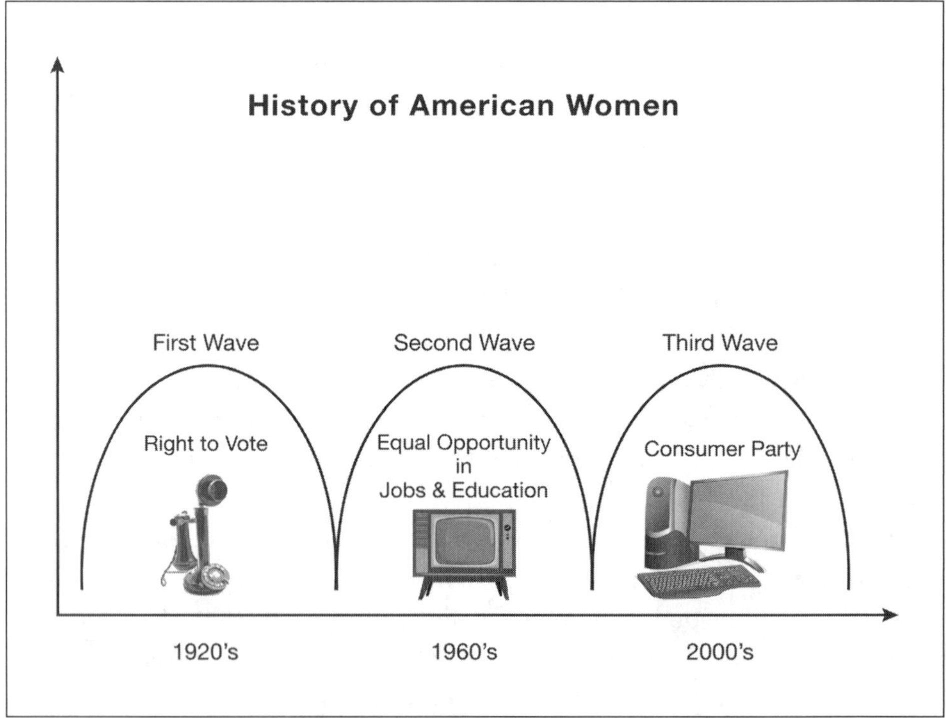

What is causing this Third Wave of feminism to spread at an epidemic rate? The emergence of a technological revolution called the *Internet.* The World Wide Web, e-mail, instant messaging—all are communication tools that play key roles in the rise of individual women for the greater consumer good.

Women are looking for ways in which technology not only works to create connections but also simplifies everyday life. Women have more discretionary income than ever, but it comes with a price: *the greater their purchasing power, the less time they have to use it.*

Women are devoting more and more of their highly valuable time to the Internet—researching, reaching out, and shopping. It fits their multitasking lifestyle perfectly, with instant access to products, services, and one another, completing a full circle in the purchasing and influencing process.

Conclusion

After watching many businesses try and then subsequently fail in the marketing to women arena, most experts agree that marketing to women as a niche only serves to undermine marketing efforts. Women are the mainstream customer base of today and tomorrow. Likewise, marketing strategies aimed at women as a general demographic see only limited, if any, success. *What really rockets businesses into the stratosphere of profitability is a marketing strategy and campaign that understands and speaks to the different types of individuals with whom they're trying to connect.*

Can you continue to market your business from the "way we've always done it" perspective and still maintain a female customer base? Certainly, until one of your competitors creates an effective marketing strategy with a message that *speaks to the individual needs and desires of a woman in a language she understands and appreciates.* Just as quickly as she appeared on your doorstep (real world or virtual), she'll vanish. Why take that chance? Why not learn not only how to attract new customers, but, more importantly, keep the ones you already have?

The perfect-storm era of marketing to women is just getting under way. The historical confluence of three factors—roles in society, purchasing power, and emerging technologies—indicate the beginning of a sea change in the way you market to female consumers. Businesses that don't sense this approaching force, aren't prepared, or think they can ignore it, risk the same fate as the legendary *Andrea Gail.*

The Third Wave is on the rise. Will you watch it roll by, or will you seize the moment, hanging ten on the cutting edge of the future?

4

Mass Adoption of the Internet:

The New Force That Empowers Female Consumers

Women have been slow to warm to the Internet. Why? Privacy concerns, technological intimidation, preference for the richer, more experiential shopping experience of the offline world. There were a lot of reasons. That's right, "were." While they may have been slow to climb on the Internet bandwagon, they are now hopping aboard in record numbers.

What changed? Websites became more user-friendly. Security concerns were addressed. Early adopters reported back with positive reviews. Once women dipped their toes in and found the water was fine, they became exponentially enthusiastic. They're not just wading in slowly; they're running and doing a cannonball off the end of the dock.

There are four converging factors that make the Internet the most powerful force for reaching women and tapping into their trillion-dollar economic clout:

- Women have dominated offline shopping, and are well on their way to dominating online shopping.
- Cultural, neurological, and societal trends make the Internet the ideal shopping source for women.

- Mass adoption of broadband has allowed the average Internet user to enjoy all the benefits of faster speed and increased functionality (video streaming, etc.), making the online experience richer and more rewarding.
- There's less time spent with traditional media outlets, and more time spent on the Internet.

All these factors spell one thing: The unequaled power of the Internet to reach and connect with women and their wallets.

Let's explore each of these factors to see why they're so important.

Women Are Dominating Online Shopping

Women accounted for 51.6 percent of Internet users in 2004. Women are 51 percent of the U.S. population. But while ratios of women in the general population through 2009 will remain steady, that won't be the case with the online population.

According to eMarketer, by 2008, females are expected to account for 52.6 percent of U.S. Internet users, outnumbering males by about ten million.

So we know women are on the Internet. Women have long dominated offline shopping. And it looks like they're going to do the same online.

Here are some other interesting statistics:

- JupiterResearch's February 2006 report forecasts that online retail spending will increase from $81 billion in 2005 to $95 billion in 2006, and will grow to $144 billion in 2010. The same report predicts that the Internet will soon influence half of all retail sales.
- In 2003 women were responsible for 60 percent of all online spending, according to a report by Goldman, Sachs & Co., Harris Interactive, and Nielson/NetRatings. Traditional female-product categories now have become the fastest growing on the Internet.

Don't think all of this money is spent only on beauty-care products and clothing.

Women are taking control of buying in sectors that have traditionally been dominated by men, like electronic gear, where women account for $55 billion of the $96 billion spent between 2003 and 2004, according to the Consumer Electronics Association. And home improvement, do-it-yourselfer women are increasing in numbers, while do-it-yourself men are actually declining according to the 2003 survey done by the Home Improvement Research Institute of Tampa, Florida.

The bottom line is, women are on the Internet, and they're spending a lot of money. The numbers are too large to ignore, and they're trending upward as we speak.

Trends in Women's Lives Fit the Internet Perfectly

Cultural, societal and Internet business trends are combining to shift the online balance toward women. Women, who have long dominated consumer shopping offline, are shifting more and more of their purchasing to the Internet.

According to a survey of one thousand U.S. households conducted by NetSmartAmerica.com, men and women surf the Internet for different reasons. The study found that most women go online to save time, simplify their lives, and to help them make smart decisions, whereas men tend to look at news, sports, stocks, and other entertainment sites. While this may be a dramatic simplification, there's still some important information here.

Another study by Neilson/NetRatings and Washingtonpost.com found similar statistics.

- Nearly seven in ten online working women with children feel they do not have enough time for their personal lives. Six in ten online working women overall feel that way. (Fewer than half of online working men say they do not have enough time.)
- Despite their lack of free time, online working women are heavy consumers of television, the Internet, and radio programming. 60 percent spend more than one hour per day online.
- About half of online working women have increased their use of the Internet in the past year—far head of any other media. At the same

time, one-quarter of online working women are *decreasing* their time with television, magazines, and print newspapers.
- When looking to save time, the Internet and radio are *least* likely to be removed from the online working women's routine.
- The Internet has become a key component of all purchase decisions, whether the transactions occur online or offline. Nearly 90 percent of online working women say they "conduct more product research online than they would be able to offline."

It's a common theme we hear again and again: **Not enough time.** But the Internet allows her to shop on *her* schedule. At eleven at night when the kids are in bed and the day's work is done, she can now shop to her heart's content. The local mall has been closed for hours, but the Internet is open for business 24/7, 365 days a year.

Choices and comparison shopping have never been easier. She can find exactly what she wants. And unlike men, women will not settle for "good enough." It's got to be exactly right. Product comparison also enables her to compare her options and find the best value. For a certain segment, hunting for the best deal is a trophy a woman wears like an Olympic medal. But be forewarned: Price is not nearly as important a factor as you may think.

Another big attraction to the Internet is **research**. Most women hate to walk into a car dealership, home improvement store, or electronics outlet and not know what they're talking about. They fully expect to be condescended to at best, and conned at worst. By doing research online, they can get answers to all their "stupid" questions, walk into the selling environment armed with knowledge and be ready to get what they really need and want. What's the difference between HDTV, a plasma TV, a flat-screen TV, and an LCD TV? Women will do their research online and have the answers they need to feel comfortable and confident in their shopping expeditions.

The Internet also affords anonymity. A website does not know whether you're a man or a woman (except if you're a returning customer and they have tracking information on you), but it will not alter its behavior even if it does know. It's an equal playing field. Tall, short, overweight, skinny, male, female, white, African American: You all get the same treatment. Do not underestimate how important that is to women.

Mass Adoption of Broadband

The growth of broadband has reached a tipping point and is a powerful driver in the increase of online advertising in the United States.

The latest estimates from Nielsen/NetRatings released on March 14, 2006, indicate that the number of active U.S. broadband users who access the Internet from home increased 28 percent year to year, growing from 74.3 million in February 2005 to 95.5 million in February 2006.

This increase in broadband also seems to correlate with an increase in time spent on the Internet: Nielsen/NetRatings also claims that the average PC time spent per person on a monthly basis also is increasing as broadband penetration rises. Its correlating estimates on this score were 25.5 hours in February 2003, nearly 28 hours in February 2004 and in February 2005, and more than 30.5 hours in February 2006.

Something else to think about: Even if she doesn't have broadband at home, she often has it at work.

With faster, more reliable Internet connections and richer online experiences, women (and men) are enjoying their time online more than ever. And they're spending more time online than ever. If you want to reach her, the Internet is a great place to do it.

Decline of Time Spent with Traditional Media

When was the last time you sat down and read a newspaper? Or do they pile up unread, only to go into a recycle bin or provide bedding for Gazpacho the Guinea Pig? When did you last sit down and read an entire magazine other than at the dentist's office? How about the radio? Or are you listening to your iPod and commercial-free satellite radio? Are you watching as much television as you used to? And when it *is* on, is it just background noise while you're doing something else?

Internet users say they are spending more time online—and less with other media. In 2005, Burst! Media discovered that more than 35 percent of respondents said they were watching less television, and nearly as many said they were spending less time with magazines. Some 30.3 percent said newspapers were getting less of their attention.

Here's more bad news for advertisers. The upcoming generation is even more skeptical about ads than their parents. They're very market-savvy and are experts at tuning out or avoiding the messages you try to push at them. It's getting harder to prove return on investment for traditional marketing efforts.

Conclusion

Many marketers are exploring other media channels in order to reach consumers. We'll go into this more in-depth in our Future of Marketing section. But for now, the one thing to keep in mind is a woman's increased time spent with digital media. Women are on the Internet, reading and writing blogs, exploring forums, e-mailing friends, and doing research. More and more marketers are turning to the Internet to explore new marketing opportunities. They're finding exciting new ways to communicate with consumers—especially women.

PART III

Understanding Gender Differences: Nature Versus Nuture

Nature Versus Nurture

One day in the not-so-distant past, a group of scientists gathered together to study how children react to unusual situations. They took a large laboratory, emptied it of furniture and hauled in a gigantic, steaming pile of horse manure.

The first subject, a seven-year-old boy, entered and immediately assessed the scene in front of him. He wrinkled his nose, grabbed the pointer from the chalkboard and began poking at the pile. "Peeeee-uuuw!" he cried as he stormed around the room. "What are you trying to do to me, sticking me in this place with a stinky pile of horse doody? Get me out of here!"

A short time later, the researchers brought in a seven-year-old girl. As the door to the room opened and the girl saw the pile of horse manure, a big grin spread across her face. With a running start, she leapt into the air and dove headfirst into the pile. "Yippee!" she shouted as she came up, dripping in horse apples. "Whoo-hoo . . . this is awesome!"

The scientists rushed into the lab. "Little girl," they said, "why are you so happy?"

"Well," she replied, "with all this horse poop, there has to be a pony in here somewhere!"

You say horse doody, I say pony. This story illustrates how one situation can be viewed from two very different perspectives. Some say it shows pessimism versus optimism; others see it as male versus female. Students of philosophy may even call it yin and yang, the two primal opposing but complementary forces that are found in all things in the universe.

Whatever your point of reference, the basis for these differences is grounded in two very real aspects of the world: *nature,* or the physical makeup of a person, and *nurture,* the environmental influence in shaping a human personality.

There's very little argument that men and women are different. Companies have made some attempt to address those differences. *We need to market to female consumers,* companies say. *We must show women that we care about them. Let's put more of them in our advertising, maybe create a "women's" section on our website. And let's repackage some of our products and talk about how they've been designed with women in mind.*

To these companies, women *are* different, and they realize they need to speak a language that traditionally hasn't been used in advertising. But that's where it ends. Most businesses fall into the trap of believing in the "ethereal woman." They see her as an intangible, emotional being with mysterious traits like intuition and nurturing behavior. Then, they build a marketing campaign around those ideas, resulting in a spongy handful of ineffectual words and images.

In reality, successful marketing to women requires an in-depth understanding of the many layers of the female consumer. It's not enough to depend on what society has taught you about gender difference. To hit the marketing to women bull's-eye, *you need to know her from the inside out as an individual.*

Consider us your guides in peeling back the layers of the female consumer. Throughout this book, we'll show you how she really is different, from men *and* from other women.

First, the foundation for understanding how women are different. Let's look at the female brain and the world that surrounds it.

5

Language of the Brain:

Women's Perspective on Life and Shopping

In order to brand your product or service in the hearts and minds of female consumers, it helps to understand some basic concepts of the female brain and exactly how all-encompassing a woman's thought process is in dealing with her world on a daily basis.

Are men's and women's brains really all that different? Until recently, there were many obstacles standing in the way of scientific exploration of gender difference. Now, recently discovered technology like functional magnetic resonance imaging (MRI) is helping major medical institutions and universities prove there are absolute physical differences in the female brain, measurable evidence that helps to explain such traits as intuition, passion, and nurturing. The female brain is simply "wired" differently. This wiring is the foundation for the way women think, reason, deduce and react.

Let's take a tour of the female brain in order to begin to understand what you need to do to start connecting with a woman *on her terms.*

Brain Basics

The human brain is divided into two cerebral hemispheres, each with its own individual strengths and purposes. The left hemisphere, generally the dominant side of the brain for everyone, is responsible for logical, linear thought. It uses language to interpret what it observes, and processes thoughts by analyzing them to create an objective reality.

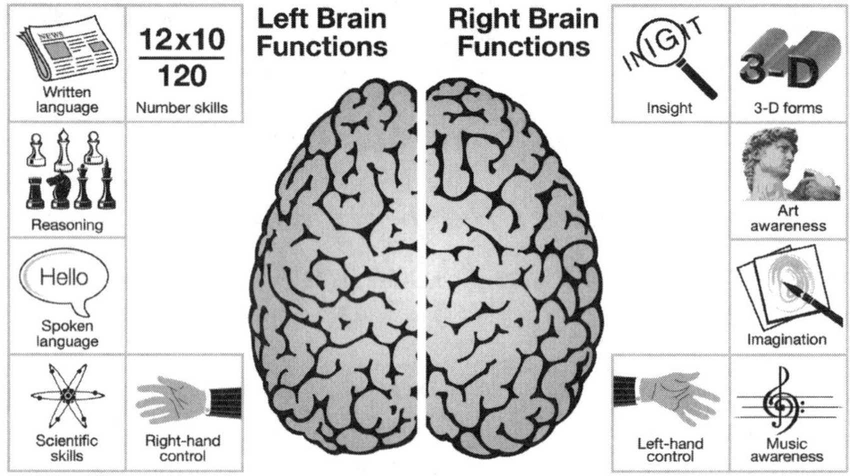

While the left brain focuses on and processes something "piece by piece," the right hemisphere of the brain works according to situational logic, taking in more information from the outside world or, as they say, "the big picture." The right brain processes a thought by supplementing it with body language, symbols, feelings, and experience. Activity in the right brain is triggered by pattern recognition—it recognizes similarities and relationships between things, rather than the differences. It is the home of imagination, and enables you to appreciate music, art, and beauty in general. It is sometimes said that the left brain is the "conscious mind" and the right brain is the "doorway to the unconscious."

Even at the most basic level, there are notable differences between male and female brains. On average, a man's brain is a bit larger and weighs about four to five ounces more than the brain of a woman. Researchers, however, focus on gray matter, that part of the working brain that allows humans to think. When measuring gray matter, women have approximately 55 percent to men's 50 percent. Women also have *four times as many neurons connecting the left and right sides of the brain.* Does this mean women are smarter than men or superior to them? No. It simply means women process information quite differently.

Introduction of the MRI: A Novel Approach

In 2000, a team of researchers at Indiana University School of Medicine, headed by Dr. Joseph T. Lurito, undertook the task of studying basic differences in the way men and women process information. Each participant was directed to listen to a descriptive passage from *The Partner*, a popular novel by John Grisham. As they listened, a series of MRIs was taken to compare brain activity. Interestingly, the MRIs of every male participant showed dominant activity in the left hemisphere of the brain, while the MRIs of the female participants indicated heightened activity on *both* sides of the brain. It was evident that the men were focused on processing the content they heard from a logical, linear perspective, while women also added nonlanguage-based processing that included emotion, imagination and experience.

These MRIs show that with four times as many connections between the left and right hemispheres of the brain, it is much easier for women to transfer data from one side to the other at a high rate of speed, as well as take in a variety of information and add it to basic objective logic. Women have what has been called a "naturally ambidextrous brain," capable of enhanced perceptual speed, fine motor skills and a higher degree of verbal fluency. This also accounts for women's ability to multitask at an extremely high level, often referred to as the "executive brain."

Thanks for the Memories

With all the extra connections between the two hemispheres, the female brain is a virtual superhighway of whole-thought processing. But what good is turbo-speed if you don't have a map to get you where you need to go? In the case of humans, that map is the right brain's collection of emotions, memories, and experiences. Women just happen to have a stronger anchor in those areas of the brain. Barraged with thousands of incoming signals from the outside world, women tend to act based on the comparison of those signals to emotional memories and experiences in addition to basic logic. This is the magic key to making your business the one a woman thinks of first and feels best about when she needs your product or service.

To illustrate how deep emotional memory is stored within each human, let's look at a recent study from Stanford University. Men and women, connected to MRIs, were shown a series of photographs and asked to rate each for emotional intensity on a four-point scale, ranging from neutral to very negative. Based on previous knowledge, it's no surprise that the brain-activity pattern of women differed greatly from that of men, with a large number of stimulated areas in both hemispheres.

Three weeks later, the participants were surprised with a second test and were asked how many of the images they could recall from the first round. Women remembered a much greater number of highly emotional pictures than did men, showing that for women, *general memories and experiences are often based on the addition of emotion to ordinary fact.*

Emotional Memory + Experience = Intuition

Emotional memory is also the foundation of intuition, one of the least understood traits of human existence. Intuition seems to bypass the left hemisphere of the brain, offering insight and accurate guesses in lieu of rational thought. An "Aha!" moment manifests itself in many ways, a "flash" of knowing or a "gut" feeling, for example. To think that intuition is ethereal and mysterious is akin to believing a magician actually makes a playing card "appear"—it's an illusion. Just as the card seems to pop out of nowhere, you're really only experiencing the end product of the intuition process. By the time a feeling hits you, your body and brain have gone through more contortions than Harry Houdini in a streamer trunk.

With four times as many connections in the brain, a woman has the ability to rapidly link and process data, pulling in all kinds of information from her surroundings. She is unconsciously accessing the file drawers of the right brain, tapping into emotional memories and feelings, sorting and looking for similarities to what she is presently encountering. The unique combination of fact, emotional memory and experience is what accounts for the strong intuition factor in the female gender.

When a female customer encounters your business, be it through advertising, in-store experience, or online, what do you think her intuition is telling her? You might be surprised . . . and you'd better take it seriously.

Her Brain on Shopping

MICHELE: I have a confession to make. I am jealous of my husband.

Sometimes, the shopping process just seems so easy for him. He decides what he wants, does a little research, bada-bing, bada-boom, he buys what he wants. And if there are some unwanted waves along the shopping expedition like there were recently with the very major purchase of a big-ticket projection television, it rolls off him like water off a duck's back.

I, however, turn it into a prime-time soap opera.

Are we sure this is the projector we want? Do we know anyone else who owns one? What do you mean it will be delivered *next week*? That's what they said seven weeks ago. Heck, that's what they said seven *months* ago! Why do we have to keep calling the store to find out the status of the order? Why don't they call *us* once in awhile? Now they want to charge us for *delivery?* How can you continue to do business with these guys? I will never, never, *never* darken their doorstep again, even if they're the last video sales guys on the planet. Wait till I tell my sister . . .

You get the idea.

How can my husband and I have such different approaches to the shopping experience? I attribute it to wiring in the brain, and think it applies to many men and women out there.

As a refresher, remember that the left brain is the logical, analytical side of the brain—it is the worker bee, focusing and analyzing one thing at a time. The right brain is free to play—it's the home of imagination, emotional memory, and bonding with others.

With four times as many connections between the left and right hemispheres of the brain, women are four times as likely to tap into the right brain when encountering a situation. Many factors come into play when going through the shopping process for women—it's all about the "big picture."

Using my husband and myself as examples, here's a simple diagram of the process my husband goes through:

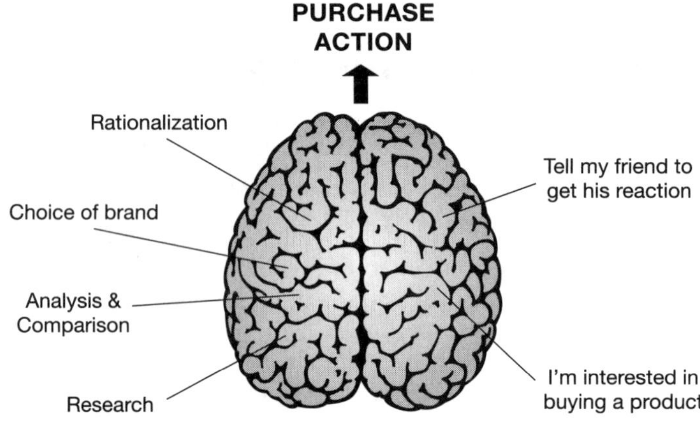

Now, here's my process:

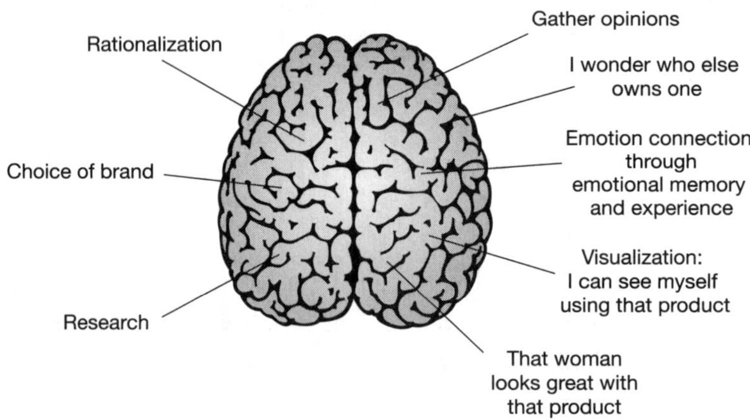

Notice how heavily a woman utilizes the right side of the brain when making a purchasing decision. She usually sees or hears about a product or service from someone else. She has to imagine herself using the product—not just how it will look but also how it will feel. She does research, but she also spends a good deal of time getting opinions from others, friends and experts alike.

In the case of the projection television, I wasn't just thinking about how the picture would look. I also thought: *Hey! This would be great at Thanksgiving, when the family comes for a visit. It means the guys would stay at home to watch the football game instead of going out to the sports bar, and the family would be all together for the entire holiday. Ah, happy, happy family.*

The language of marketing to women is based not only on words but on so much more, including signals from every one of the senses, emotional triggers, intuition, and the respected opinions of others.

But it doesn't end there.

There is one more critical piece to the puzzle that brings it all together for her. It's called "The Halo Effect":

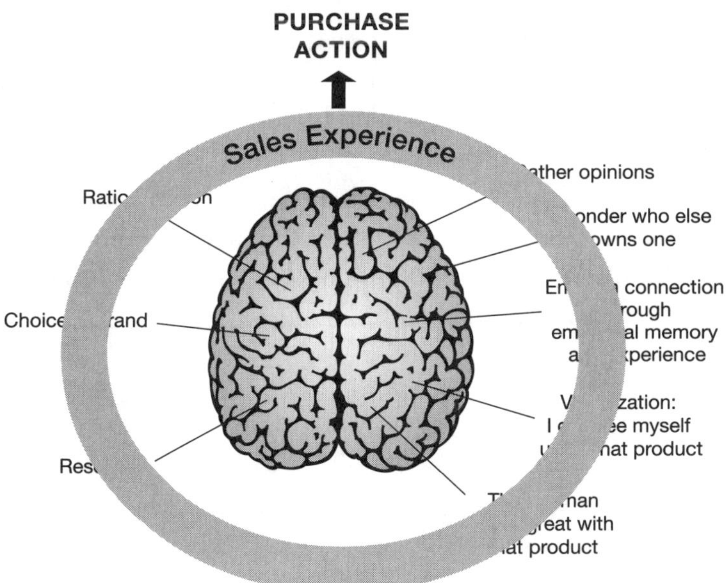

Her experience with your store or business is the tipping factor in whether she's going to do business with you. What constitutes an experience? Everything. There are hundreds of touch points. She considers the convenience of your location (or ease in finding you on the Internet); the size of your parking lot; the atmosphere of your store (or design of your website); how your employees answer the phone; how customer service treats you as an individual, whether it be in-store or online—no matter how much money you spend; how management handles problems, both real and virtual; and on and on.

Conclusion

Do men also tap into the right brain during the shopping process? Definitely—some more than others, but rarely as much as women do by virtue of the wiring in the brain. For her, the experience is the halo that pulls everything together—it can make or break a shopping decision. It also affects the probability of her becoming a repeat customer, not to mention a brand champion. And if she has a poor experience with your business, God help you. You can expect her to divulge the entire saga to those she knows. With women three times as likely to relate an experience, good or bad, to a friend, the halo effect reverberates far beyond the individual noggin.

For women, it's all about connecting—connecting with you, your business, and connecting her with others. It's up to you what kind of connection you will make.

Today, most marketers talk about branding from the aspect of "having a place in her heart." Could it be that most campaigns fall short because they've targeted her heart when they should have been aiming a little higher above the neck?

6

The Nurture Side of Gender Difference:

How Society Plays a Role

In January of 2005, Harvard University President Lawrence Summers suggested that an innate difference between men and women might be one reason there are fewer women in the fields of science and engineering. More than fifty Harvard professors signed a letter protesting his statement, and alumni threatened to withhold donations. Summers has since apologized. But were his statements founded in the truth?

Do men and women differ in mathematical ability? If so, where do the differences come from? Biological differences, as we've seen, have been scientifically proven. Boys do better in terms of certain brain functions like visual spatial skills. But is that enough to explain the disparity?

What else might be at work? Gender stereotypes? Cultural bias? Some studies show girls tend to be less confident about their abilities in math than boys. Does this have an effect? What about the toys each sex is encouraged to play with? Little girls get dolls, boys get to build things. And what part do teachers and other adults play? Are girls discouraged from pursuing an interest in math and science? Does the lack of female role models play a part?

In the early nineties, Teen Barbie, a talking version of the doll, proclaimed "Math class is so hard!" Talk about perpetuating a stereotype. No other toy in history has had a greater effect on expectations of women than Barbie. An activist group, the Barbie Liberation Organization, bought Barbie dolls and G.I. Joe dolls, then swapped their voice boxes, so macho G.I. Joes squealed, "Let's plan our dream wedding!"

Bias and gender stereotypes aren't just perpetrated by men. Women play a role as well. A large part of the problem is that people are often unaware of their bias. How can they deal with it if they don't even realize it exists?

Historical and Cultural Conditioning

Since the beginning of time, men and women have traditionally played different roles. Men were the hunter-gatherers, the providers, the solo explorers. Women were the caretakers. They raised the young, were responsible for caring for the home and the family, and worked together with the other women as a community.

We've seen brain differences that give women an advantage in verbal skills. This, combined with their innate sense of community and sharing, leads them to place greater value on relationships.

> *The vast majority of studies show women outperform men in language tasks and produce speech more easily and fluently. . . . This love of conversation, and our ability to use it to strengthen relationships, is one of the great joys of female friendship. My friends don't make points; they tell stories. . . . Men, on the other hand, stick to the facts and often groan or roll their eyes when their wives launch into a long anecdote.*
>
> *Why Men Never Remember and Women Never Forget*
> —Marianne J. Legato, M.D., F.A.C.P

Men's historical reaction to stress has been to handle it on their own. They are conditioned to "go it alone." Men have been trained not to show or share their feelings. Many women have traditionally responded to stress by reaching out and bonding with other people, often other women. Laura Cousino Klein, Ph.D. and Shelley Taylor, Ph.D. at UCLA have been studying this response. They've found men have more "fight or flight." Women have a different response they call "tend and befriend."

Conclusion

Combined with wiring in the brain, historical and cultural conditioning results in some very pointed differences in how genders process and act on information. In the next chapter, we'll look at how some of these differences affect the ways in which women communicate and make decisions and how that affects your marketing efforts.

7

Gender-Based Communication Styles:

How They Differ and How They Affect Marketing

HOLLY: On Heather's refrigerator is a drawing of a mustachioed stick figure standing next to his motorcycle and boat, with the caption "My Fiancé." Instead of being the work of a three-year-old, it is the work of a forty-three-year-old. Why this strange refrigerator ornament? Blame it on a high dose of cortisol combined with male versus female communication style.

Ever wonder why after arguments men seem to get over it more quickly? Ask them what the argument was about and they barely remember. Women, on the other hand, tend to feel the wounds of arguments more deeply. They can often repeat every word that was said. There is a biological reason for this—cortisol. When women are stressed, their bodies release cortisol, and it stays in their system longer—which tends to heighten and lengthen the period of stress.

After such an argument, Heather ripped down all the pictures of her fiancé and threw them into the trash can. It was only an impassioned plea from a close friend crying "Not the good jewelry!" that kept several pieces of expensive jewelry, including the engagement ring, from following the pictures into the jaws of the Suburban Sanitation truck.

After an extended period in his "man cave," Heather's fiancé came back and was ready to continue where they'd left off. From his perspective, the argument was not a big deal. In *his male communication style*, conflict is a normal part of how couples communicate. Distressed that his picture was no longer anywhere to be seen in the house, the fiancé expressed his hurt and disbelief that all of his pictures had been ripped to shreds.

Heather, in her more *female communication style,* came away with a totally different interpretation of the argument. She looked at it as a breakup of the relationship. It took a lot of back-and-forth for both of them to come to an understanding of what had really transpired. Once both parties cleared up the miscommunication, they were able to move forward.

Thus, in the spirit of reconciliation, the stick drawing now adorns the refrigerator for all to know that the fiancé is indeed back in Heather's good favor. Every time he walks into the house, he can rest assured seeing the mustachioed stick man smiling back at him. When the fiancé started adding little muscles to his stick arms, Heather knew the relationship was once again on the road to recovery. With any luck, actual photos will once again adorn the walls.

Even today, ask this couple about that blowup and you'll find he looks at the argument as a blip on the radar screen, while she looks at it as a near relationship ender.

Believe it or not, this same scene plays out with companies and brands, not just fiancés. She has a bad experience with your company or product. You think, *It was just a customer service call, she couldn't get her questions answered and had to wait ten minutes to get a live person, that's just a blip*. But to her, it's a relationship ender. What to you may seem like small things can be huge to her.

Male Versus Female Communication

Men and women have differing communication styles. No surprise there. Just look at all the relationship books focused on helping each gender understand the communication style of the other. How and what you communicate is absolutely key to persuasion.

Whether you are a husband who wants to convince your wife to have another child or a marketer who wants a woman to buy your product, what you communicate and how you communicate it will determine your success in reaching your goal.

Men's and women's differing communication styles are based both in science and nature. Biological factors as well as evolution have created different strengths and weaknesses, different priorities, and different values in each gender.

As the ancient hunters and gatherers, men were often put into a position of competition. They were competing against nature while trying to hunt and capture dinner. They were competing against one another for tribal status and mates. Winning, whether in a fight against an animal or a fellow tribesman, meant staying alive.

Women, on the other hand, were often put into a position of cooperation as the family caretakers. They would band together to help with child care and other domestic duties. For women, avoiding fights meant staying alive.

That history still affects us today. Men are competitive and hierarchical. They establish rank and status. Women look for similarities and value cooperation.

In their book *Why Men Don't Listen and Women Can't Read Maps*, Barbara and Allan Pease quote an interesting study. This study, conducted in five Western countries, asked men and women to describe the kind of person they would ideally like to be. Men overwhelmingly chose adjectives such as *bold, competitive, capable, dominant, assertive, admired,* and *practical.* From the same list women chose *warm, loving, generous, sympathetic, attractive, friendly,* and *giving.*

Understanding what each gender values can have an effect on every communication you have with your customers. If you want a man to respect and trust your company, you may want to stress the adjectives he uses to describe what he admires. If you want to win the respect of women, you may want to consider using the adjectives she uses to describe qualities *she* admires.

How do you handle conflict? Have you noticed men and women handle conflict differently? Many men, especially in a business setting, resolve conflict by *escalating* it. They take a strong position and argue it until one of the two parties involved gives in or submits to the other. Many women resolve conflict by *de-escalating*. Rather than focusing on differences, they focus on common ground and finding compromises.

Men try to differentiate themselves. Women look for points of similarity. Look at something as simple as a conversation at a cocktail party. You have a group of guys and a group of women who don't know one another. The guys' conversation may go something like this:

> *"Great weather today. I went out and played eighteen at The Links."*
>
> "It was a great day. I played thirty-six."
>
> *"Have you played The Rivers course yet? I played there last weekend, expensive, but well worth it."*
>
> "Yeah, I play there all the time. It's a fun course. But The Boulders puts it to shame."
>
> *"I shot my best score ever at The Boulders—a seventy-eight."*

Men respect hierarchy and establishing status. Now let's look at a typical conversation between two women who don't know each other.

> *"So, Samantha, do you have any kids?"*
>
> "Yeah, a four-year-old, Zach, and Amy was born four months ago."
>
> *"Four months ago? And you look terrific! Did you gain much weight during the pregnancy? I gained thirty pounds and still haven't been able to take it off."*
>
> "I gained a lot of weight with Zach. So this time I signed up with a personal trainer at my gym. She specializes in fitness during pregnancy. I felt great!"
>
> "*You know, my best friend, Andrea, is pregnant. I'd love to tell her about this trainer. Do you have her information?"*

Women seek common ground. Often, women's natural instinct is to help one another. Plus, they can often discuss what might seem like very personal information almost right away. Where men may focus more on facts, women focus in on personal details, but only if they feel like it is safe. We suspect women may be quicker to trust because they rely on more senses to judge people.

Women have the ability to detect a wider range of emotions than men. Men can detect straightforward emotions like rage and aggression, but women can pick up on subtler emotions. In the case of women, this could be due to the greater number of connections in their brain. It could also be that in the role of a nurturing mother, a woman is required to pick up on the more subtle emotions of her baby in order to understand its needs.

> *It seems that a woman can tell if something is wrong with her child, a parent or a spouse as soon as she lays eyes on them, while men can easily miss even the most blatant signs of distress.*
>
> *Why Men Never Remember and Women Never Forget*
> —Marianne J. Legato, M.D., F.A.C.P

So how do a woman's need to connect and a man's need to establish hierarchy affect what and how the two sexes communicate? They determine which messages and communication styles will be more effective with each sex. In other words, it affects which marketing messages resonate with each sex.

This is not to say that women don't appreciate and crave status. But how you communicate that need for status may need to be framed in a different way.

Take a recent television commercial that shows two trucks squaring off. One truck springs a leak and figuratively "pisses" on itself. This is a very male communication of status. It's about hierarchy. One truck is the clear winner.

Another television commercial shows a mother dropping her son off at school in the family Hummer. Seeing the cool car, the boy's peers greet him with immediate acceptance. This commercial also promotes status, but in a more female communication style. It takes a more communal angle, with the focus on the fact that it is the son as well as the mom who benefits from that status.

Car commercials are an easy target because so many of them are testosterone driven. Start with hard-driving music (a la Led Zeppelin), show a car/truck/SUV driving really fast around sharp turns or going ultra-rugged on a mountaintop or steep trail. End with a strong male voice-over making a bravado statement. Very male communication style.

Compare that to the Lexus "December to Remember" commercials. These are all about gift giving. (Women are natural-born gift givers. We'll be talking more about this later.) The commercials are focused on people and their stories. In one, a man is at a jewelry store where he's feeling really uncomfortable and is not sure what to buy, when he looks out the window and sees a car that appears to have a red bow on it. In another, a woman is shopping online (imagine that!) for a holiday present, when she looks outside and sees a car with what appears to be a red bow on it. The people are the stars of these commercials. The focus is more on the reaction of the gift receiver than it is on the car.

Or look at the Volkswagen Passat ad. It is a dark night on a curvy mountain road. You might think this is another typical car commercial. But then you see the car encounter a biker without a headlight. The Passat driver follows the biker, guiding the way down to the bottom of the winding road, where streetlights can now light the biker's way. It is a guy driving the car, but this is a much more female communication style, highlighting how you can use this cool headlight feature to help someone else (as opposed to bragging about it to your friends).

HOLLY: I recently talked with a friend who was in the market for a new car. She'd driven Hondas all her life and loved them, but she wanted to try something different—maybe just a little more upscale. When I asked her what cars she was considering, she had it narrowed down to three: A Volvo, a Lexus, or a Volkswagen Passat.

Who says advertising doesn't work?

Quick note: Lest you think men will be turned off by commercials with more female communication styles, look at that Lexus commercial with the guy in the jewelry store. It is a commercial firmly targeted at guys. He wants to get her something really special for the holidays and thinks jewelry is what he's supposed to get. But he's horribly uncomfortable in the jewelry store. He looks up at the stone-faced, sophisticated jewelry store saleswoman and gives a weak smile but tries not to make eye contact. How many guys feel uncomfortable as hell in an upscale jewelry store? Think they can relate? When he looks at the car outside, you can see the relief on his face. "AHA! I can go to a car dealership, a place where I'll feel much more at home, and buy her a car." He's just as thrilled by her reaction when she sees the car as she is.

How Our Differences Affect Marketing

OK, enough of this nature and nurture scientific stuff. What are the actual differences that affect how we market to women online and offline?

> *Men and women are said to demonstrate different ways of interacting, expressing emotions, playing games, having a conversation, handling authority, giving and receiving instructions, initiating friendships, reacting to problems, establishing connections, relating to hierarchies, appraising situations, and taking control. Men are more likely to be separate, individualistic, oppositional, thinking in terms of binaries, whereas women show greater "connectedness" and orientate themselves empathetically towards others.*
>
> *Created or Constructed? The Great Gender Debate*
> – Elaine Storkey

Women differ from men in many ways. It's even suggested we are so different we must come from different planets! But how do all of the above-mentioned factors affect marketing? They all affect how men and *how women shop*. These differences affect what information each gender is looking for, how they want to receive that information, in what order they want that information, and how they process that information. Let's look at some of the differences.

Expressing emotions. How do women feel about your product? What outlets do they have if they feel positively? What if they feel negatively? Women actually remember stressful, negative events more than men. Do you give your website visitors and offline customers a way to give you feedback? And what do you do with that feedback? There are specific steps you can take not only to listen to your customers but to let them know you *heard* them. And most importantly, there are ways to harness the most powerful marketing on the planet, word of mouth. There are even ways you can take a negative event and turn it into a positive.

Having a conversation. What language do you use in your marketing material and on your website? Are you writing copy that truly speaks to a woman in her own language, which creates a dialogue? Or are you preaching at her with a bunch of corporate techno-speak? A website visit truly is a dialogue. Each click is a question. Are you answering her questions? She can either enjoy the conversation or tune you out, walking out the door with her mouse.

Reacting to problems. What's your customer service like? Handle a problem professionally and take care of her needs, and she's a customer for life. Don't address her problems, and she'll not only never come back; she'll tell all her friends not to come back either. How do you handle error messages on your website? Are you making her feel stupid? BIG mistake. You can create error messages that address the problem without placing any blame. What are her objections? Are you addressing them or avoiding them?

Giving and receiving instruction. Take a look at your website navigation. Are you giving her obvious clues where to go and what to do once she gets there? Do you have clear, strong calls to action? What about your website check-out process? Do you spell out exactly how many steps are involved and what's involved in each step? Are your forms intuitive and only asking for the information you absolutely need?

Establishing connections. What are you doing to create a relationship with your customer? Are you treating all your customers the same? She wants to feel special. She wants to know you genuinely care. What kinds of cause marketing are you doing? Slapping a pink ribbon on your door and saying "We support breast cancer" isn't going to do it. (Note: Breast cancer is a wonderful cause. We're not diminishing its importance, but we do believe that too many corporations pay lip service and don't really do anything that's truly different or meaningful.)

Ethical practices. Some research shows women are more ethical than men. This could be due to a combination of biological brain wiring that allows them to see the big picture, and societal pressure on women to "always do the right thing." Harvard University's Carol Gilligan wrote about it in her book *In a Different Voice*. The *Los Angeles Times* headline of 2002 announced "Women Are More Likely to Blow Whistle" after a series of high-profile women blew the whistle on major institutions like Enron and Worldcom.

Whatever you do, do not be deceptive in your practices or copy! Deceptive e-mail headers may get high open rates but low conversion rates. Once a woman feels she's been deceived, her opinion of your ethics goes down the tube, no matter how tempting the offer. Do not promote something as "free," then in fine print tell her that she actually has thirty days to try it and if she doesn't return it, her credit card will be charged $79. You need to make this kind of offer very clear. Even if she likes your service, if she feels you've deceived her in any way, she and her credit card will walk away, AND she'll tell others of your "unethical" practices. What you're doing may be completely legal, but often ethical is in the eye of the beholder.

The bad news is, there are a lot of differences you need to take into consideration when you're truly trying to reach and understand your female customers. The good news is, if you take the time and make the effort to really do it, your reward could be a rocket-fueled leap ahead of your competition and a big fat a la mode piece of a trillion-dollar pie.

The LPGA: Swinging Like a Girl

HOLLY: Here's one societal difference between the sexes that affects sports marketing. Women value relationships and rapport; they have a nurturing nature, seeking solutions based on the common good. Men value competition and individual accomplishment. Many men like to boast of their achievements.

What do you do in a sport like golf, where the emphasis is on the individual's achievement? Look at the LPGA. Their "I Swing Like a Girl" promos feature several powerhouse players looking soberly at the camera and saying, "I swing like a girl," then show a close-up of them knocking the snot out of a ball.

I get where the LPGA is going with this ad. Players today like Michelle Wie (only a teenager and drives the ball almost three hundred yards), Annika Sorenstam, and others have made names for themselves not only by their talent but by the power with which they play. Swinging like a girl, which was once a derogatory comment, can now be considered a compliment.

But I don't believe the ads entirely work. The players look slightly uncomfortable when they're saying, "I swing like a girl." We don't know what emotion the players are supposed to be feeling as they say the line "I swing like a girl." Is it tongue-in-cheek? Then why do they look so serious? Is it bragging? That's probably closer to the truth, but it feels and looks unnatural for these players, especially golfers, who are more discreet and humble than many of their sporting counterparts. These women just don't look entirely comfortable bragging.

Imagine how the whole feel of the spot would change if instead of the players saying, "I swing like a girl," you heard the voice of a young boy taunting, "You swing like a girl" as the players swung for all they were worth. Wow, now *instead of bravado you have solidarity.* What woman hasn't at one point in her young athletic life been taunted by some pipsqueak saying something just like that? Now, at the end of the promo the players can look straight at the camera with a knowing look and say, "Yeah. . . . I do." Take THAT, you snot-nosed pissant!

How else could you create promos that speak to the ability of the players and the intense competition without bragging? The LPGA created one of the best promos of all time, in my humble opinion, when the great rivalry was raging between Annika Sorenstam and Karrie Webb. The promo featured the two players on-camera, jovial and joking, saying they really liked each other and there was no deep competitive rivalry. But after each exchange, the promo would cut to a scene of one of the players secretly trying to sabotage the other. The final shot was of one of them slapping the other on the back and saying what good friends they are. As the two walked off down the fairway, away from the camera, you saw a sign that said "Kick Me" on one of the player's backs.

That ad was brilliant in many ways. It accurately portrayed a very real and deeply competitive rivalry, but by approaching it from the viewpoint of "We're all friends" and taking the tongue-in-cheek attitude, it made the point without the players having to brag or boast.

Conclusion

What's your company's communication style? What is the communication style of your advertising message? Are you paying attention to the details? Are you recognizing the importance a woman places on everything you do? Remember, what may not seem like a big deal to you could be a relationship breaker for her.

In the coming chapters, we'll take a closer look at your messaging and how to speak your customer's language.

PART IV

The Power of Marketing to Women as Individuals

Women as Individuals

MICHELE: A few months ago, I was driving to the Austin International Airport, a little behind schedule but determined to make it in time for my flight home. As I tooled along Route I-35, a Volkswagen zoomed past.

At first, what intrigued me about the little white VW Bug was the bumper sticker, which read GIRLS WHO DON'T MISBEHAVE RARELY MAKE HISTORY. Curious, I sped along to catch up and spied a young woman in her late twenties, dressed in office attire, singing along with the radio. The VW pulled away, but I just had to know what kind of flower the woman had in the Bug's vase. I hit the gas, pulled alongside, and peered through the VW's window.

There was no flower at all. It was an American flag.

Into what kind of marketing category would you try to pigeonhole this woman? Is she a hippie? Corporate wench? Young college grad? New mom? Conservative, or liberal?

You already know that when it comes to marketing, women require a different approach simply by virtue of wiring in the female brain and the influences of society and culture. It's a good start but still a rather broad-based way of viewing it, don't you think?

Remember the ethereal woman, that intangible, emotional being with mysterious traits like intuition and nurturing behavior? Oftentimes, in order to more narrowly define the ethereal woman, marketing executives believe they'll add depth to their campaigns by creating "categories" of female customers. You're probably familiar with some of these groups, which include fashionistas, graying grannies, and the ubiquitous Soccer Mom. Based on demographic information and cultural generalizations, advertisers believe these groups give them everything they need to know in order to target specific markets.

The problem is, typical categories still aren't enough when it comes to marketing effectively to women. In fact, they don't work at all. We're entering an age when those categories are starting to break down, losing their power in the first stages of marketing entropy. For example, we still hear the term Soccer Mom bandied about, but motherhood isn't what it was ten years ago. Women are waiting longer to have children; some have important corporate careers, while others work from home. The narrow demographic-based definition of a Soccer Mom doesn't account for today's overlap of age or different value systems. So who exactly *is* the Soccer Mom?

Female consumers are beginning to say, "Enough already. Time to recognize me as an individual—not by demographics but by what I carry around via the inner self."

Have you taken a long, hard look at your current customer base lately? Not from the perspective of zip codes and income but, rather, values and needs?

Perhaps it's time to start looking for clues of an overlapping value system among generations of women in order to see who your customer really is. Begin comparing your customers by what they carry inside rather than what you see on the outside. Peel back another layer on the ethereal woman, and you'll quickly realize there are actually *dozens* of women underneath, all with specific needs and desires.

Only then will you be able to identify what your business offers that resonates with a woman, and make it easier to create customers for life.

8

Shattering Stereotypes:

What They Are and Why They're Harmful

HOLLY: I get very enthusiastic about my sushi. While at a recent "all you can eat" sushi outing with my sister and some friends, we ordered up a storm. As soon as my plate of caterpillar roll, yellow tail and scallion roll, and Toro sashimi arrived, I dove in. A few minutes later, I came up for air, lifting my head from my empty plate, and remarked about the poor size of the portions.

As I looked around the table, everyone else still had half to three-quarters of a plate of food. The friend to my left commented on the soy sauce dribbling from my chin and the pieces of rice sticking to my cheek. My sister pronounced I was not allowed to eat sushi in a dating situation.

What does all this have to do with stereotyping? Everything. The owners of the sushi restaurant had eyed me on this "all you can eat" sushi night and figured I was the person they'd make money on. Being a woman and somewhat small in stature, they were much happier to see me than a large man, figuring I would eat a roll or two and be done. They were sorely mistaken.

This is one of the single-biggest dangers of stereotyping: You label a person based on a few qualities. I am a woman, I am not big, and therefore I was labeled as not being a big sushi eater. Not true.

We All Stereotype

We all know her. You've seen her in advertisements. She's in her mid-thirties to early forties. She drives a minivan. She lives in the suburbs. She has a husband who means well, but she's the one who's really in charge. Her life is focused around her kids, doing their laundry, driving them to the ball field, juggling housework and cooking duties. Her days are filled with important choices like choosing the right soft drinks, finding laundry detergent that gets stains out, buying breakfast cereal that's healthy but which the kids will actually eat. You have a clear picture of her in your head, right? She's a Soccer Mom. There are millions of her out there. She's a prime target for advertisers. There's just one problem: *She's a stereotype.*

Are there women with these traits? Yes, there are. Are there women who make these same choices? You bet. But what we see portrayed are stereotypes. Stereotypes make sense because they are largely based on truth.

So what's the problem? Why is stereotyping bad? If it's based largely on truth, it lets you understand your audience better, right? And it helps you group your audience into segments that make sense. Where's the downside?

There *is* a downside, a big one. By stereotyping, you may not have a deep-enough understanding of who your customers really are, what they really want, or how to communicate with them. The lives these women live are so much deeper, richer, and more complicated than what the Soccer Mom stereotype would lead you to believe.

In past elections, a big emphasis has been placed on "The Soccer Mom Vote." I was always curious as to what that was. Are Soccer Moms considered traditionally Democrats or Republicans? Are they conservative or liberal? Since they are moms, is education their number-one priority? Since this group seems to vote en masse, how do you craft a message that appeals to them all?

Let's meet three Soccer Moms:

Sharon

- Life-long Democrat
- Pro-choice—it's my body, stay the hell out of my personal life
- Outgoing
- Married with one child

- Full-time job in pharmaceutical sales
- Loves to travel, hike, and go on adventures
- Hates to cook
- Hates guns and refuses to have one in her home
- Gadget freak—has the latest BlackBerry, iPod, satellite radio, supercool laptop
- Despises George Bush

Corrine

- Independent
- Thinks too many women use abortion as a method of contraception but doesn't think the government should control this issue
- Introverted
- Divorced with two children
- Works in the district attorney's office
- Has a permit to carry a gun (and usually does)
- Loves spending time with her two sons, likes staying at home, and always has a home improvement project going
- Indifferent to technology—uses it to make her life simpler and knows basic functionality
- Doesn't like George Bush's foreign policy but likes his pro-business stance

Lisa

- Republican
- Pro-life—believes abortion is taking a human life
- Community leader—runs a local nonprofit
- Married with three children
- Gourmet cook
- Hates technology—her husband programs her cell phone for her

- Likes George Bush because of his strong morals, pro-family agenda, tax cuts, and willingness to fight for what he believes in

So, you tell me. What political message would you create that would resonate with all three of these Soccer Moms? Are they all going to agree on the same candidate? Do they all have the same priorities? They may look almost identical demographically, but psychographically, they couldn't be more unlike.

That's the problem with stereotyping: You see a group of people who share some common traits—middle income, suburban moms, love their kids—and by trying to tie them all up in a neat little bow, you make assumptions that are often not true.

What Exactly Is a Stereotype?

Let's take a look at what a stereotype really is.

ster·e·o·type *n.*

1. A conventional, formulaic, and oversimplified conception, opinion, or image.
2. One that is regarded as embodying or conforming to a set image or type.

Stereotypes of women in the media abound and not just in advertisements. You have only to look at prime-time television to see stereotypes. In the 2002 Miami University article "Primetime Stereotyping: Social Psychological Effects on an Impressionable Culture," authors Pamela Davis, Lisa Russell, Amber Ruth, and Robert Woods discuss stereotypes.

> *If I were to tell you that I resemble a hippy woman from the sixties, you would definitely be able to come up with a mental image of me, right! Flowers in my long, flowing hair, a tie-dyed T-shirt, and bell-bottom pants. I am a free spirit, and an open-minded Liberal.*

Perhaps the description helps you get a mental image of myself. By creating such mental pictures and having a preconceived notion of what a hippy looks like, and what characteristics he or she has, you are using the cognitive shortcut called stereotyping. We utilize stereotypes in everyday life to reduce the amount of information we need to analyze. Our world is so complex that we need to categorize who and what we come into contact with on a daily basis.

People tend to use stereotypes to "fill in" details about a person if that person is not a member of their in-group, and if they do not possess the motivation to get to know them on a more personal basis.

What's the downside?

Stereotypes are shortcuts that may prevent you from doing the important, in-depth research that's necessary to truly understand and communicate with your customers.

So, how do you overcome stereotypes of women? And specifically, how can you overcome stereotypes of women who are shopping online? That's the billion-dollar question.

Here are some examples of how stereotypes can be harmful:

Look at retiring baby boomers. When you look at stereotypes of retired people, you think husband and wife, been married forty plus years, love to visit their kids and grandchildren, live in Florida, eat dinner at 5:30 at Denny's, play bridge with their friends, relax, and enjoy their newfound leisure time.

Look at ads targeting retired people and you'll see images of gray-haired couples dancing on the beach, riding in golf carts, sitting on the patio with other gray-haired couples.

Let's say you're a financial services company targeting these retired people. A typical ad shows couples like those described above doing all these wonderful leisure activities with copy that says something to the effect of "You've worked hard your whole life. Now's the time to finally sit back, relax, and enjoy your hard-earned success."

Here's where that stereotype gets you in trouble. According to futureofchildren.org, women are outliving men by seven to fifteen years. Divorce rates are still fairly high, and while men get remarried, many women are choosing to remain single. Younger women are more likely than older women to remarry, but age is not associated with remarriage among men. In other words, as they get older, women may be dating or have a full-time partner, but they are NOT remarrying at the same rate men are. The result? *There are a lot of retiring baby boomers who are single women.*

How do you think they feel when all the financial services ads they see portray nothing but older couples, or worse, older men?

While stereotypical couples want nothing more than to move to Florida and play golf, bridge, and bingo all day, the truth is, today's retiring baby boomers are more active than ever. They're going back to school, traveling, starting out on a second career, starting their own businesses, and finally finding the time to dedicate themselves to serving others through volunteering and other pursuits and occupations. (This is especially true of women.)

Imagine if you're that sixty-five-year-old woman who sees nothing but the typical financial services ad. What would happen if you saw this ad from Lincoln Financial Group? It's titled "Volunteer."

The ad features a sixty-something woman, shown with a stethoscope around her neck, standing in a small village and helping young African children. A voice-over announcer says, "Will you spend your retirement in a comfortable chair, watching the world go by . . . or will you be out there with your sleeves rolled up, changing the very shape of it?" The video ends with the woman sitting alone on the beach, gazing out into the waves. The final voice-over ends with, "Say hello, future."

Wow: THAT was different. And our guess is that's exactly how that sixty-something single woman retiree feels when she sees it. Here is a company that understands her deepest motivation in retirement isn't to sit out the rest of her life on a golf course. She wants to participate and make a difference in the world. She still has skills that are of real value to the world. She's not thinking about the end of her life: She's thinking about the start of a new one.

We can just see the executives in a typical boardroom watching this ad and saying, "No, wait! She's sitting all alone on that beach. This is going to remind women that their husbands are dead, or they're all alone in the world. What a horrible negative image. We can't show that."

What they're missing is that, to women, the image is not necessarily negative. Sure, this woman may miss her husband, but that's not what you see in her eyes.

You can tell by the look on her face that she is at peace. She is not responsible for anyone but herself. She may be alone, but she's contributing and feeling more connected with the world than ever before.

Advertisers are focusing almost exclusively on the younger consumer. Look at broadcast networks competing for the "coveted" eighteen to forty-nine demographics. It's actually considered a *bad* thing if your number of viewers over the age of fifty increases. Why is it a crime to have viewers over fifty? Baby boomers are retiring with a tremendous amount of wealth. And they're spending it! People are getting remarried and having children in their forties. That fifty-year-old viewer whom networks are so anxious to get rid of just might have three kids under sixteen in the house. And because she's had more time to build wealth, she could be spending twice as much money on those kids as her thirty-year-old counterpart does.

By making assumptions based on yesterday's stereotypical demographics, many advertisers are missing a key opportunity to reach a market that has *beaucoup* bucks, and fewer competitors targeting them.

Mother: The Most Stereotyped Woman in Advertising

From the Happy Homemaker to Soccer Mom to Super Mom, almost no other demographic has been so stereotyped as that of mother.

Ignoring the complexity of motherhood is offensive to women. They do not want to see commercial after commercial that pigeonholes them into one big stereotype.

Here's something to think about: According to the 2001 study by the Population Resource Center, 27 percent of all households are headed by a single woman. Yet the majority of today's advertising still shows the traditional mother/father household. The traditional family unit may not be as reflective of reality, but it's a whole lot more comfortable territory for advertisers.

By catering to stereotypes, advertisers stay in safe territory and don't run the risk of possibly offending someone. But the result is, there are entire genres of mothers who feel advertising doesn't speak to them at all.

While we're at it, how about stereotypes of dads? How many sitcoms have the bumbling, doofus dad and the smart, savvy mom (*Everybody Loves Raymond,*

King of Queens, According to Jim, etc.)? You see the same thing in advertising: Dad messes up dinner or the laundry, but never fear, mom will come to the rescue. Where are the commercials with just a dad and his son or daughter having a real, loving interaction? They are out there, but you don't see them very often.

The Dangers of Oversimplifying

Stereotypes are dangerous because they oversimplify. They don't allow you to see into a woman's (or anyone's) deeper needs and motivations. And you often miss entire segments of your audience by speaking to the average person instead of speaking to individuals.

In the online world, websites have a unique advantage because they can be designed with different pathways and experiences for specific audience segments. By developing personas that incorporate the varied lifestyles, needs, motivations, and buying processes of each of your audience segments, you can address each in the manner that will appeal to that specific audience.

Age Doesn't Tell the Whole Story

HOLLY: You really should meet my aunt Judy.

Aunt Judy is in her eighth decade on this earth. To look at her on paper, or even in person, you'd probably see a stereotypical older person. She lives in the conservative Midwest, she's a widow, she loves her kids and grandkids, and she's very involved with her church. She likes to play bridge with her friends. She's had some health problems, so she can't get around the way she used to. (She looked so longingly at me when I told her I was going for a bike ride my heart ached.)

But if you got to know Judy, you'd see a different picture. In her eighties, and never being even slightly inclined toward technology, you'd think she'd avoid computers and everything high tech. Not necessarily so. She has a nice computer at home and e-mails her network of family and friends on a regular basis.

Cell phones? Hers is nicer than mine, and I have a pretty impressive cell phone. When sitting down and looking at all the cool features, I noticed her phone had a welcome message programmed in that said something to the effect of "Be kind and courteous to all." I asked if she was happy with the message or if there was something else she'd like her cell phone to tell her every time she turned it on. She thought for second, then remarked she'd like the message to read "You look skinny."

Pop culture? We were sitting at the dinner table and my mother was saying how there were different goddesses for different times, and our particular time now was all about the goddess "Lady Liberty." Judy raised her eyebrows and deadpanned, "You mean it's not Paris Hilton?"

Beware of stereotypes. Do not oversimplify or underestimate your audience.

Make Your Message Stand Out by Breaking Out of Stereotypes

We saw earlier how Lincoln Financial Group is gaining women's attention by creating commercials that break out of stereotypes. Here's another example from, surprisingly enough, a technology company.

How many commercials have you seen where the husband, traveling for business, checks in with his wife and kids at home? Dozens? Hundreds? How many commercials have you seen where a woman is traveling on business and checks in with her husband and kids? Hundreds? Dozens? Three? One?

Logitech Quick Cam broke away from stereotypes and created just such a commercial. The television commercial features a traveling mom in a hotel room saying good night to her husband and kids by using video calling through her computer. Instead of just a phone call, she now has a much more interactive experience, where she can actually see her family. The voice-over stresses Quick Cam's ability to help people "make a better connection."

All too often, marketers assume it is the man who is doing the business traveling. Wake up and smell the frequent flyer miles. Women are traveling at an exponentially growing rate. Womentraveltips.com claims women now constitute almost 50 percent of all the business travel in the United States and spend $175 billion on fourteen million trips annually. This subtle nod from Logitech to female business travelers is a powerful customer relationship-building technique.

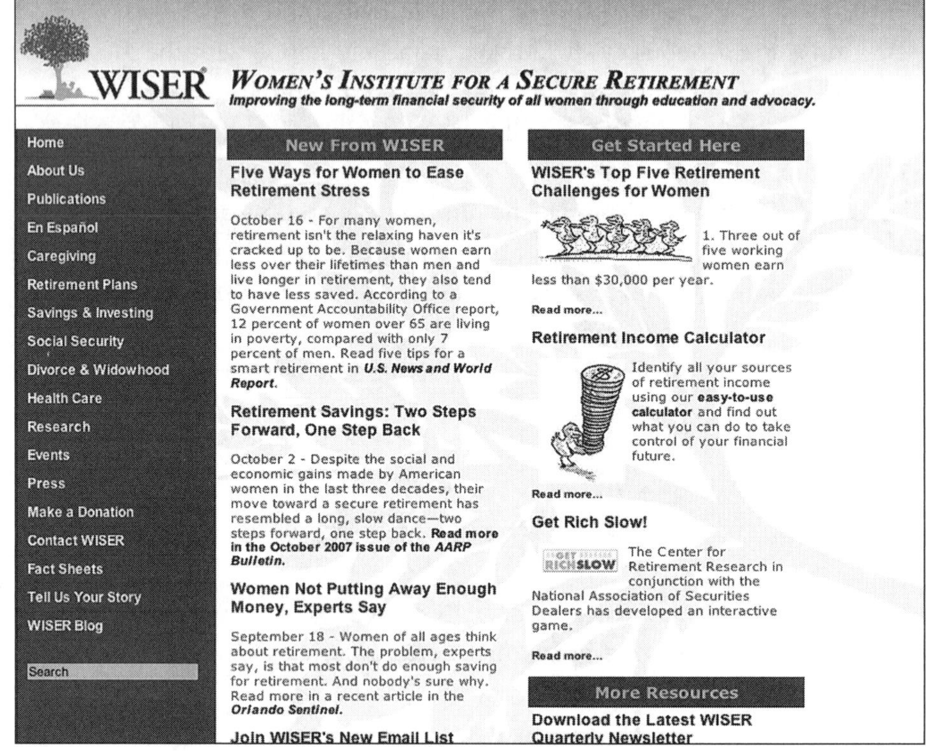

Women's Retirement On the Web

Many companies and websites want to promote their retirement plans to women. They have attractive lifestyle images, and discussions about annuities and other investment options. But it takes more than just a "feel good" picture to engage a woman and start a relationship with her. You have to talk about what *she* cares about in her language.

The Women's Institute For A Secure Retirement (WISER) does a nice job of talking to women about issues they care about. There are no beautiful images or fancy design elements, just text talking about what women researching retirement are interested in.

The copy acknowledges that women's thoughts about retirement have changed. Women today are starting second careers, going back to school, volunteering. They care about long-term care and the unique challenges they face as women. By addressing these concerns and providing links to valuable information and resources, WISER is building trust and rapport with their visitors. Isn't that what most financial services websites are trying to do? Perhaps they should take notice.

The Other End of the Spectrum: Girls Fifteen to Twenty-five

When you think of most fifteen-year-old girls, you probably imagine somewhat immature but fun-loving girls whose only interests are fashion, boys, and the latest gossip about who-dumped-who. You probably picture them barely managing an allowance or working at some part-time job at McDonald's or a mall boutique.

You probably wouldn't picture them living in New York City, having more talent and marketing know-how than advertising professionals three times their age, helping to run a hot up-and-coming marketing agency, and working with huge brands like Unilever, Playtex, and Jones New York.

But it's true. Yup: Fifteen-year-old girls. Sound crazy? You won't think so after you read about Holly's conversation with Heidi Dangelmaier, founder of 3iying, an all-girl marketing agency.

HOLLY: 3iying specializes in marketing and design strategies for girls fifteen to twenty-five.

It takes a lot to impress me in the brains department, but Heidi is just scary smart. She is a self-described "girly scientist" who was the only female robotics student in the Princeton Ph.D. program. She went from the world of science to the world of video games to the world of marketing. She is an inventor, and she has used her scientific background and innovative imagination to create a company that can consistently come up with relevant, new ideas that resonate with their target audience.

3iying doesn't just specialize in marketing to girls whose age range is 15 to 25; the women who make up the company are in the same age bracket. After talking with Heidi, I think there are four reasons for the company's success:

1. **The creative directors, designers, and strategists are themselves the target audience**. Their bullshit meters go off the moment any sort of messaging isn't authentic.

2. **They focus not on *what is*, but on *what could be*.** Traditional advertising is based on statistics, or what is known. 3iying focuses on innovation, or what could be. They look for holes, for unmet needs, for new angles, all of which are based on what consumers want, not what companies want.

3. **They have a process**. Because of Heidi's scientific background, 3iying uses a proven process for their research, testing, and messaging. They aren't just relying on creativity. They have a repeatable formula for success. Strategy always comes first.

4. **Uncorrupted talent**. Because 3iying is based in New York City, Heidi has unusual access to the best and brightest from area schools. The girls she hires may be young in age but not in skills. They are one talented bunch and share an international background. Heidi makes a point to contact these girls before they get out into a traditional agency setting. She wants to reach them before they are forced to give up their natural instincts in order to conform to the more traditional, and often male-dominated world of advertising.

I asked Heidi how she and her young "girl think tank" get respect from big-name companies and billion-dollar brands. She feels it's because advertisers and companies are more willing to admit they don't know what younger girls want. With older women, they think, *Hey, I have a wife, so I know how women think.* But fifteen to twenty-five-year-olds? They're more open to the idea that this group is harder to peg or understand. So they're coming to 3iying for insight they feel they don't have themselves.

Smart move. Those companies are reaping the rewards with new products, brands, and messages that are creating fans in this hard-to-impress age group.

Conclusion

Whether you're talking about mothers, aging baby boomers, teenage girls, or anyone in between, resist the temptation to stereotype. Resist the temptation to treat them as if they are all the same. Make the extra effort to really reach out to these women, immerse yourself in their lives, take the time to talk to them about what keeps them up at night, and where they find their greatest joys. The deeper you probe, the more successful your efforts will be.

9

Maslow's Hierarchy:

The Foundation of Understanding How to Market to Women

It's too bad Sigmund Freud never met Abraham Maslow. A couple of good conversations with Abe might have cleared up that whole "what women want" thing for him.

In the midst of his quest to answer the psychological question of what women want, Freud threw up his hands in the late 1800s (perhaps a little out of despair) and declared, "Anatomy is destiny." In other words, women were born to get married, have babies, and take care of the home.

Quite a stereotype for an entire gender to follow, don't you think? But for a number of years after World War II, this was exactly the message projected to the American woman. Advertisers told her happiness was in a bottle of floor wax—those gleaming linoleum tiles reflected the smiling faces of her children. Fulfillment was watching her husband relax in front of the fireplace after a long day at the office, with delicious smells of dinner wafting from her state-of-the-art kitchen.

It got so out of control that Betty Friedan, author of the 1960s manifesto *The Feminine Mystique,* took advertisers to task for maneuvering Freud's theory to an even darker side: "The practice of psychoanalysis as therapy was not primarily responsible for the feminine mystique. It was the creation of writers, and editors in the mass media, and ad agency motivation researchers . . ."

Thankfully, advertising has "come a long way, baby." But businesses still struggle to get a grasp on exactly what women want and how to give it to them. You're now aware of the tradition of stereotypes that exist out there and you're ready to break away from the pack by addressing the individual needs of women. But where to start? What's a business to do? Perhaps, as Abe would tell us, the question isn't exactly what women want but what they *need* and *when they need it.*

Maslow's Hierarchy of Needs

If you've ever taken a course in psychology, human behavior, or education, chances are you've heard of Abraham Maslow. Born in the early 1900s, Maslow studied human behavior extensively, focusing on what he believed to be the most important factor in the development of individual happiness: The satisfaction of particular needs in order to strive for more in life. The result of his work was Maslow's hierarchy of needs, which he illustrated as a pyramid:

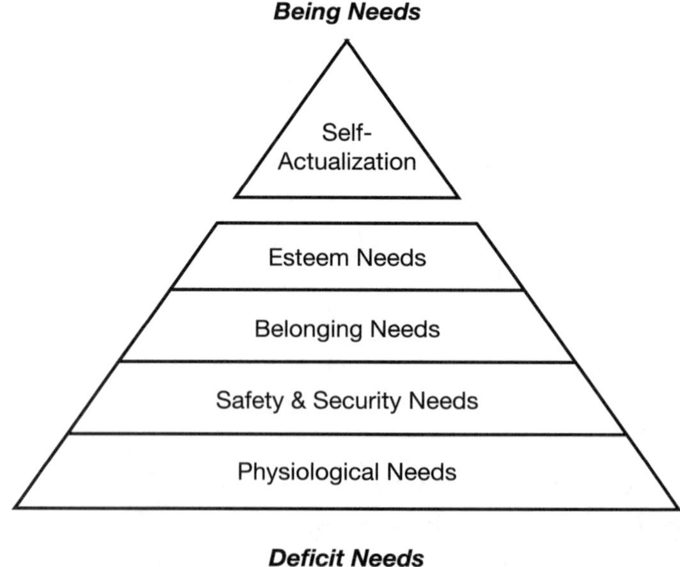

Maslow saw that a human being's needs must be met from the bottom up. The most basic needs, *physiological,* are those required to sustain life like oxygen, food, and water, for example. Next are the *safety* needs like security, shelter, etc. These are followed by *belonging* needs including love and acceptance, and *self-esteem* needs like confidence and self-worth.

A human can only rise to a new level of need when the current level has been satisfied. She can (and will), however, descend to a lower level depending on a sense of deprivation. Maslow compared it to a furnace thermostat—when it gets too cold, the thermostat turns the heat on; when it's too hot, it turns the heat off. Needs change all the time and human beings are self-regulating.

At the very top of the pyramid is the "being need" of *self-actualization*, that small percentage of humans (about 2 percent of the population) that focuses on the world outside itself. This is the woman who has a clear sense of who she is yet is still very connected to the world. She experiences peak moments of love, understanding, happiness, and feeling alive. She has a strong connection to truth, justice, and brotherly love. This is the ultimate state of being, that level that Maslow believed many of us dream of but few actually achieve on a consistent basis.

With a simple yet profound theory of human behavior, Maslow showed it's nearly impossible to split a population into demographic categories for marketing purposes. Generalizations about graying grannies and Soccer Moms just won't work because there are too many variables, the most important being an individual woman's need at any given moment. Take a group of Soccer Moms and try placing them on Maslow's pyramid. They'll be scattered from top to bottom. Each mother, depending on the life experience stamped into the right side of her brain and the environment in which she lives, is going to have a separate, individual need to fulfill.

Volvo Listens to Women

A highlight of the 2004 European auto expos was the unveiling of Volvo's YCC (Your Concept Car), a prototype created by an all-female design team. Rather than focusing on one specific target group, Volvo set out to discover and meet the needs of individual women drivers. The elegantly futuristic vehicle boasts gull-wing doors and an electric-hybrid engine that needs an oil change only after thirty-two thousand miles. It has run-flat tires, allowing the driver to get the car to a garage after a puncture rather than be stuck on the side of the road. The interior has extra storage, removable textile panels to change color schemes, and headrests with indentations to accommodate ponytails.

Executives at BMW and General Motors pooh-poohed the concept, but Volvo CEO Hans-Olov Olsson claims they missed the point. It was never Volvo's intention to build this car for mass consumption, he claims; rather, it was to find out what women wanted and incorporate those solutions into future Volvo vehicles. Olsson added, "We learned that if you meet women's needs and expectations, you also exceed those for men."

Maslow and Business

Maslow knew his hierarchy of needs could be applied to many areas beyond psychology, including business. He saw its importance in every aspect of enterprise, from determining the goals of the business owner, to hiring, training, and nurturing staff, to building relationships with customers. Maslow believed that, using the hierarchy of needs, there are some simple steps a business could take to propel itself toward greater profitability:

1. Build your business to outlive you.

Maslow gauged the character of a business owner or manager by asking, "Do you want this company to grow even after you're dead?" Ask yourself the same question. Whether you retire, die, or even sell your company, do you give a damn whether it thrives without you? Passion and caring for something outside yourself is a characteristic of self-actualization and provides a rock-solid foundation for building a profitable business.

MICHELE: Everything you do should be done with the idea that the show will go on even if you're not around. I remember an important lesson learned from Robert C. Jones, a vice president of the Kennedy Center for the Performing Arts. I was working at Sirius Satellite Radio and found myself in the middle of a heavy-duty negotiation with the Kennedy Center for exclusive broadcast rights to all performances. Bob kept sending back the contract with what I felt were frustratingly minuscule details. When I questioned him about it, he replied: "Michele, this is a very important event we are negotiating. You and I both have to do everything we can to make sure we've set this deal up for a time when neither of us is around." He was so right. It was one of the biggest lessons I've learned in business.

2. Fulfill the needs of your staff first and watch your business grow.

While you pay people to work for you, it is your responsibility to do everything you can to fulfill a certain level of need for your employees. What is it you can guarantee you'll do for them? Decide which level of need you have the ability to satisfy. For some businesses, it's a basic level of safety and security in the workplace; for others, it's the creation of community and sense of belonging to a special kind of organization. Whatever it is, make sure they know you are committed to fulfilling this need, then do so on a consistent basis. If you achieve this, your turnover rate will drop dramatically and your employees will begin looking for ways to strengthen the business on their own.

Remember, once an individual has her needs met, she strives for a higher level. The key to Starbucks' success has been the belief that employees come first. Chief executive Howard Schultz understood very early on that everything a Starbucks' employee does in front of a customer matters, "Happy employees make happy customers." He also realized he had to satisfy the needs of employees in order to retain them. From extensive training to stock options and health coverage for part-time employees, Starbucks has done what it can to provide for the welfare of employees and in doing so has built a multibillion dollar company.

3. Determine which level of need your product or service fulfills, then deliver.

Once you have happy employees, how do you make your customers happy? By figuring out what level of need your product or service satisfies and doing everything you can to make sure it happens. Be confident you can choose a level you know you will be consistent with and are fully capable of delivering.

Let's say you sell automobiles. You spend some time thinking about the women who visit your dealership every day and try to evaluate what most of them are looking for. After working on it awhile, you decide that what your female customers want most is a safe, reliable vehicle. It's then up to you to do everything you can to make that the heart of your message. Talk about safety ratings in your advertising; on your website, have a chart comparing the safety records of your car to the competitor's. Make sure the dealership lot has extra-wide parking spaces to allow more room for maneuvering and less worry about other drivers. Give a free class at your dealership every Saturday, teaching women how to safely install a child's safety seat into their automobiles. Your focus should be on anything that has to do with safety and security. Your middle name should be "Safety." There are myriad ways to resonate with a specific need, which translates not only into sales but also into customer loyalty.

4. Look at what your competitors are doing, then kick it up a notch.

Often, average businesses satisfy a certain level of customer need without even thinking about it. Average advertising (usually a sale of some kind), average product, average customer service. Depending on the competitors in your town, this may be enough to make you the big fish in a little pond. But if competition is fierce and you want to stand out, what do you do?

Easy. Take a look at how your competitors market themselves. What level of need on Maslow's hierarchy do they focus on? Figure it out, make sure you do everything possible to satisfy that need, and then market yourself one level higher. Remember, once an individual has had her needs met, she will strive for a higher level. Why not be the business to offer it to her?

Marketing and delivering on higher-level needs are what some producers of the most powerful brands in the world are masters at doing. While Volvo focuses on safety and security, BMW is all about "the ultimate driving experience." Dunkin' Donuts sells coffee; Starbucks is a place to commune with friends and colleagues, a "third place" of belonging. Dell sells solid, reliable PCs; Apple fanatics belong to a unique tribe devoted to design, style, and forward-thinking ideas. All of these "superbrands" aimed their sights a little higher on the hierarchy of needs and have carved out a mega-position for themselves that few can challenge. They are well-positioned, focused, and deliver exactly what they promise on a consistent basis. To the customer, these brands are irreplaceable.

Conclusion

Once you've tried "the hierarchy of needs" techniques above and they begin to work, you're bound to respond by saying: "This is great, but I know there's more to this Maslow stuff. You've already told me not all women have the same needs, especially not at the same time. Isn't there a way I can be talking to *all* of them?"

Congratulations. You've entered the realm of Third Wave thinking, marketing to women as individuals rather than an amorphous gender. There *are* ways you can start connecting with women who need your product or service, all for different reasons. But it requires a level of work and commitment for which you must be prepared.

Don't worry. We're not talking about creating ten thousand marketing ideas in order to reach every woman on the planet. We're here to make it a little easier for you by providing a powerful method known as *personas.*

10

Personas:

The Key to Marketing to Women

We've talked about the dangers of stereotypes. But how do you go beyond stereotypes? How do you gather information about women that goes beyond demographics and surface-level needs? How do you really get to know your female customers?

Here's a key: **You have to understand a woman in the context of her whole world**. Women lead very complex and very integrated lives. They don't get up in the morning and put on their mother hat, then take that off and put on their career hat at work, then take that off and put on their wife hat when they climb into bed with their husband. A woman wears many hats all at once (a true fashion challenge).

The more you understand how a woman really lives and what's truly important to her, the more you'll be able to deliver a meaningful message. That's why personas are so powerful. Personas give you insight you can't get from raw data. They let you break down hundreds of thousands of customers into a few "real" people. They let you understand your audience based on who people are and, more importantly, *how they buy.*

So, what exactly are personas? Glad you asked. You may have heard the term before, but at Future Now Inc., we have our own definition of personas and methodology for creating them. The commonly accepted definition is "An archetypal representation of an actual user group whose members share similar needs and goals."

- Personas are developed using real data and research about real people.
- A persona is not based on a single customer, but, rather, on a group of customers with similar characteristics.
- Personas are complete pictures that include demographics, bios, needs, motivations, objections, and buying preferences. And that's just the beginning.

More and more companies are using personas for everything from designing new software, to product development, to crafting marketing messages, to creating entire shopping experiences. At Future Now Inc. we use personas to do all of the above and more. For a more in-depth explanation of personas, you may want to read *Waiting For Your Cat to Bark* by Future Now Inc. co-founders Bryan and Jeffrey Eisenberg. But we'll try to give you a simple overview here.

Why are personas so powerful?

- They give you insight into how people use your products.
- They give you insight beyond just surface-level needs, revealing deeper motivations.
- They give you an understanding of what questions your audience is asking.
- They give you an understanding of different buying processes, so you can match your selling process to the way someone wants to buy.
- They give you an understanding of how customers think and what words they use to describe their problems (think keywords).
- They help pinpoint possible objections: In other words, what's keeping her from taking the action you want her to take.

That's just the beginning. For this book, we'll focus on the **three most important aspects** of what you can gain from personas:

1. What your customers' deeper motivations are;
2. What questions they are asking;
3. What heir objections are.

We'll delve more deeply into those three aspects in the following chapters.

Sample Personas

Let's say you're creating a website promoting cruises to women. Sounds like a pretty narrow audience. You've done a lot of research on your customers, and here's what you've found out. Your customers are professional women ages twenty-five to fifty-four, with household incomes of $100,000 and up, and families with an average of two children. The one thing they are looking for is *escape*. Great. All useful information. There's just one problem. One type of customer is an extroverted go-getter. She loves challenges and makes decisions quickly. The other type is an introverted, quiet woman who doesn't like to be rushed. She likes to do a lot of research and take her time when making a buying decision. Even though these women look exactly the same on paper, they approach the buying process in very different ways. Plus, different women have very different visions of what "escape" looks like.

So how do you create a website that addresses a variety of customers with different needs and different buying processes? You create personas.

For this website, we've created four personas: Mary, Helen, Connie, and Susan. Note: These are actually what Future Now Inc. would call "profiles." Our normal persona process would go much more in-depth. These are more simple profiles than fully fleshed out personas. Your personas should be much more in depth. But we've simplified these personas for the purpose of this example.

Mary: Mary is a CPA. She is a planner. She buys her Christmas gifts in August. Her children's lunch boxes are neatly packed and ready to go the night before. She prides herself on her ability to hunt down bargains. Mary's idea of a good time is curling up with a cup of green tea and reading mystery novels. Mary is slow to make decisions. She gathers lots of information so that she can feel completely confident in her decision. For Mary, escape means sitting in a lounge chair on the deck of a ship with a cup of freshly brewed iced tea by her side and a stack of her favorite books ready to dive into.

Mary will plan her cruise six months in advance. She will methodically research every cruise available on the website. She will pay attention to every detail. She will research the ships and the destinations. Getting the best value (not necessarily lowest price but the best value) is important to Mary. The purpose of Mary's cruise is rest and relaxation. She will book well in advance.

Helen: Helen is the assistant human resources director for a midsize company. She was recently promoted at work because of her listening and people skills. Helen lives for her family. She values relationships above everything else in her life. She is active in her church and in her children's school, and her house is a favorite with the neighborhood kids because they always feel so welcome. Her idea of escape is gathering a gaggle of girlfriends and laughing and sharing stories and experiences.

Helen wants to go on a cruise with nice people. She's looking for a cruise with cooking classes so she can learn to make new dishes for her children. Helen will be slow to make a decision. She will browse the site and look at cruises that will make her feel good. She'll respond to testimonials that let her know what kind of experience others have had on such a cruise. She'll want to find out who the crew is. She will enjoy images with lots of people laughing and enjoying one another's company.

Connie: Connie is one of the top-performing sales reps at a pharmaceutical company. She is a competitive, type A personality. If she's not active, she's not happy. Connie makes decisions quickly once she feels she has the information she needs. She likes to compare all her options, and she values competency above all else. She is constantly exercising her mind and her body. She does yoga, hikes, and works out at the gym. She loves to travel and experience new cultures. She is constantly pushing her kids to get involved in lots of activities that will let them expand their minds and tackle new challenges.

Connie wants the best cabin the cruise offers. She wants a cruise line with a reputation for outstanding service. She wants to go to an exotic location, one she's never been to, so she can learn about a new culture. She also wants a cruise that offers a lot of fitness activities so she can work on her abs and lose a few pounds. She is looking for a cruise that offers seminars on finance and other subjects, so she'll know she's making the most of her time. Her idea of escape is the freedom to experience as many different, self-actualizing activities as she can.

Susan: Susan is fun-loving and spontaneous. She thinks people who live to work are missing the whole point of life. She is a graphic artist and her "work" is all about self-expression. She freelances because she does not want to be tied to a corporate schedule or lifestyle. Susan loves to go out to dinner, shop, and attend concerts. When the new spa opened up in town, she was the first one to try the "hot stone" treatment.

Susan will decide where she wants to go at the last minute. She'll check out the activities each cruise offers. The more the better. Susan is looking for fun. Susan likes the personal touch, like a bathrobe in her room and a bouquet of flowers ready for her arrival. Can you say shopping? Susan lives for shopping and spas. Price is not a big factor.

These women all look the same on paper, but they approach the buying process in very different ways and are looking for very different things. To accommodate them, you need to understand how your customers approach the buying decision. Most websites focus on the selling process rather than on the customer's buying process. The disconnect between the two means lost opportunities and sales. In order to understand how your customers reach buying decisions, you really have to know your customers and help guide them on their own individual paths through your website.

So, how do you do that?

Let's start with **Mary**. We know she is looking for a lot of information. You want to send her to a page that lists all the different kinds of cruises and their destinations. Mary is a planner, so provide a page that talks about "What to Bring" or "What You Need to Know Before You Board." We know Mary likes to book in advance, and value is important to her. So, on the page giving information on the type of cruise/destination, you would include a link to a page that lists special low prices for those who book in advance. By providing a link with a call to action (Book in advance and take advantage of early-bird specials) that clearly provides information that is of interest to Mary, you propel her forward in the buying process.

Helen wants a cruise that will let her feel more connected to people and the universe. She wants to build experiences and connections. She wants to feel good about herself. So send Helen to a page that lists cruises designed to help her become all she can be. She'll respond to testimonials that let her know what kind of experience others have had on a similar cruise. Include bios and pictures of the crew. She will enjoy images with lots of people laughing and enjoying each other's company.

Connie is looking for new experiences and challenges. Send her to a page with cruises to exotic locations. Include a link to another page, one that lists all the activities on those cruises. Include a link with information about the fitness facilities on board. Be sure to include copy that informs her of anything unique about the cruise, the ship, or the destination.

Susan will be attracted by a page that lists last-minute cruises, cruises that still have space available, and are set to sail within a few weeks. Susan will also be interested in a page that discusses how your cruises provide the personal touch. Once again, provide a call-to-action link on the last-minute cruise page that sends her to the personal touch page which will explain how this particular cruise will be special. Provide momentum to keep Susan clicking and moving deeper into the site.

All four women may travel from the Home Page to the "Book Now" page, yet each will get there by her own path, driven by her own interests and buying needs.

Seeing the Whole Person

Can you see how understanding the whole person gives you insight? In *Beyond Listening, Learning The Secret Language Of Focus Groups,* author Bonnie Goebert says it perfectly. "Take the blinders off clients so they can see buyers as whole people, not just the end point on a decision tree about salad dressing choices. With a deeper understanding of the entire human being, marketers can fine-tune their message, make advertising more relevant and products more meaningful."

HOLLY: Take this example. I got an e-mail one day from a man who was selling an all-natural cleaning product. It was healthier and less toxic than other cleaning solutions, and it really worked (or so he said). An obvious market for his product was environmentally conscious people who clean. But if he had done personas based on women who clean and looked at their whole lives and other priorities, he might have found out something interesting. What do a lot of women care about? Their skin. If we know a woman cares about her skin, how can we tie that need/problem/opportunity to this cleaning product? We can do it with the following copy:

> *When you are in the shower, your skin is at its most vulnerable. Thanks to the heat and steam, your pores are wide open, soaking in everything around them. Do you want those pores soaking up fumes from your toxic shower cleaner? Save your skin with the all-natural, less harmful fumes from the organic cleaning product.*

Conclusion

Creating personas is one of the most powerful techniques you can use to truly understand your customers, not only how they are similar but how they are different. By looking at a woman's whole life, you can identify new opportunities to meet her needs. You may discover very powerful messages you might not have thought of otherwise.

11

The Three Most Important Dimensions of Personas:

How Motivation, Questions, and Objections Make a Persona Who She Is

There are many dimensions to a persona. You can dig really deep and create personas that are rich and recognizable. They can have full life histories and complex buying processes. For our purposes in this book, we're going to look at three of the most important dimensions of personas: Her deeper motivations, the questions she is asking, and her objections.

Deeper Motivations

There's a famous advertising story about the Betty Crocker company back in the days of June Cleaver. Betty Crocker looked at women's needs. The company recognized that women didn't have as much time as they'd had in the past to bake. The advertisers saw a chance to meet that need and to take advantage of a clear marketing opportunity by creating an instant cake mix that would be much quicker and easier than making a cake from scratch.

The company worked diligently until they developed a formula that simply required adding water. Perfect, right? Yet women didn't respond to the product the way Betty Crocker had hoped. Why? Because it made a woman feel less accomplished. It took away the pride of baking the cake. Betty Crocker didn't take into account the *deeper motivation* of why women bake.

If it were just a need for dessert, a woman could run out and buy something from a store. Her deeper motivation was the love, accomplishment, and pride she took in baking the dessert herself. Just adding water made it feel like cheating.

So what did Betty Crocker do? The company reconfigured the formula, requiring her to add an egg. NOW it felt like real baking. It's been a huge success ever since.

We talked earlier about Maslow's heirarchy. Different companies and products target different levels of Maslow's pyramid. The higher the level you target, the more likely your product is to make a strong emotional connection. So try to look beyond surface needs to deeper, more self-actualizing motivations that may really be driving a woman's purchase.

Some cookware is marketed to the consumer's need. You've seen the nonstick surface frying pans and easy-to-clean-up baking dishes. But many of the high-end cookware manufacturers have figured out a woman will pay a lot more money if you appeal to her deeper motivation. They dig deeper and find out that she wants to be a gourmet chef. She wants to impress family and friends with her cooking abilities. She is proud of her kitchen and the top name-brand utensils within it. Kitchens used to be hidden in the back of the house. Now they are front-and-center showpieces. "Non-stick" may allow you to charge $25 a frying pan. "Showpiece gourmet cookware" allows you to charge $250 a frying pan (and up).

What are some other examples of deeper motivation?

- She doesn't just want an air freshener to cover up odors—she wants her house to have a pleasing smell.
- She doesn't just want the container for her windshield wiper fluid in her car to be obvious so she can refill it—she wants to feel competent and confident about her ability to care for her car.
- She doesn't just want to be able to play golf well with her male colleagues—she wants to be respected and treated as an equal, on and off the course.

If the most important motivation to her is respect, which headline do you think will perform better, "Play better golf," or "Get the respect you deserve on the golf course"?

If she's really all about confidence and independence, which headline speaks to her, "Clearly marked windshield wiper fluid containers," or "You'll never have to ask for help to fill your windshield wiper fluid container again"?

Think about our cake example. Which would be a better message, "Serve them a fabulous dessert," or "Show them how much you love them"?

Diamond companies get it. Take the enormous popularity of the "Three stone ring," which represents past, present, and future. The companies don't say "Get her a fabulous anniversary gift." They say "Tell her you'd marry her all over again." It isn't really about the diamond; *it's about the deeper emotion it represents.* (OK, if it's a beautiful multi-carat rock in a stunning platinum setting, it's about the ring. But it's still the love as well as the bling that makes her heart sing!)

Personas are wonderful vehicles for determining deeper motivations. As Paco Underhill observed in *The Science of Shopping,* "The obvious isn't always apparent." By having a deeper understanding of her whole life, you gain an understanding not only *how* she uses your products but *why.* When crafting your marketing messages, if you can speak to her deeper motivation your message will have much more of an impact.

What Are Her Questions?

What questions are your customers asking? Do you know? Are you answering their questions?

Take a thirty-eight-year-old mother of four. She has a big family. She does A LOT of laundry, but she genuinely loves her family and takes pride in a job well done. Her question is, "Is there a towel that can be washed day in and day out but still remains soft?"

Most towel companies say their towels are soft, but do they remain soft after multiple washings? Lands End answers her question.

> *Unlike "Treated Towels" Ours Start Out Soft and Become Softer with Every Wash. Lots of towels are coated with chemicals to make them*

> *feel soft on the store shelf. But wash them a couple times and their softness goes down the drain. Not ours! Because we use better cotton and superior construction, our towels get plumper and softer with every wash; Guaranteed.*

If she were on a website and saw a link that said "Choose a towel that remains soft through lots of laundering," do you think she'd click on it?

Lands End goes on to describe the towel further, which is great. You always want to back up your claim. But most website product information would start with this copy, it's typical features/benefit copy you see everywhere.

> *We use only the top 3 percent of cotton grown in the United States. Farmed for its extra-long, strong fibers, Supima cotton feels softer, lasts longer and pills far less. Start with better cotton and you end up with a better towel.*

Most companies are so focused on their selling points, they fail to answer her questions. You can give her your selling points once you've answered her questions, but **always answer her questions first.**

One of the primary ways in which women use the Internet is for research. We cannot stress this enough. You must provide copy that gives her the information she is looking for, whether it's a website, a product brochure, or a direct-mail piece.

Let's say you have a woman who has a growing business. She's moving out of her home to a real office. She's hired fifteen people and needs a phone system. Her questions are:

- What are my options? What phone system will work the best for an office my size?
- What about voice mail? Or conference phones?
- Can I add more phones if I hire more people? How hard will that be?
- What features do I really need? I want to keep costs down.
- What about installation?
- Who's the best company to deal with?
- How much is it going to cost?

Most websites provide copy like this:

> *XYZ business phone systems are next generation converged IP-PBXs that offer superior functionality and a low cost of ownership for single and multi-site businesses. Each of our phone systems is a highly scalable and complete IP-PBX offering cost effective Voice over IP enabled solutions for any sized business.*
>
> *The XYZ product family supports logical stepped increments of 25, 50, 100, 200, and 300 users per chassis, including support for T1/E1/PRI high-capacity trunking. We have the ability to continue to expand by networking multiple sites or systems together (local and remote chassis networking) for higher capacity or multi-site implementations.*
>
> *These exceptional scaling and networking capabilities are the hallmarks of XYZ's Distributed Intelligence Network Architecture (DINA).*

Huh? Chassis? High-capacity trunking? Intelligence Network Architecture? This copy makes some very weak attempts to answer one or two of her questions, but the answers are so full of techno-speak the answers are not clear.

Here's copy from another site. Think they do a little better job of answering her questions?

> *A phone system is one of the most important purchases your business can make. The telephone is often the easiest way to reach your customers, clients, and partners. It should also be the easiest way for them to reach you. You do not want your important business callers to be routed incorrectly, disconnected, or faced with a bewildering array of automated options.*
>
> *There are many factors to consider when buying a telephone system. For example, you need to get enough capacity for your current needs while planning for growth.*
>
> *You will want to ensure compatibility with other equipment you already own or may need such as voice mail, messaging on-hold, headsets, or conferencing equipment. And you will need to choose a phone system that supports all the features your business requires.*

Managing all of those factors while keeping costs down can be a huge challenge, but XYZ can help. This Buyer's Guide will help you understand the types of decisions you need to make and how to choose a phone system.

Types of Phone Systems

- *Sizing a Phone System*
- *Basic Telephone System Features*
- *CTI and Advanced Features*
- *Office Phones Dealers*
- *Office Telephones Pricing*
- *Buying Tips*

This copy is written in plain English, it addresses almost all of her questions, AND the company provides links that answer each of her questions.

Let's take another example. A woman is shopping for her apartment. She wants an area rug that will match her furniture, be durable, and not stain. She wants a more natural look. She is drawn to the Natural Fiber rugs. She surveys the different types: jute, sisal, seagrass, but they all look the same to her. Most of the websites she goes to have a picture of the product and some sort of terribly non-helpful information.

One example:

100% pure natural jute, non-skid backing with a 100% 2-1/2" cotton binding.

Just showing her the pictures does not answer her questions. Her questions are:

- What the heck's the difference between jute, sisal, and seagrass? They all look the same. I see some price differences. Does that mean one is better quality than the others?
- Is one of these more durable than the others? Can they handle a lot of traffic?

- Do they stain easily? If my friend Jan comes over, I know she's going to spill her red wine. Is it washable?
- How does each rug feel? They look a little coarse. I like to walk barefoot in the summer.

If she searches around, she may find some websites include more helpful information:

> ***About Jute***
>
> *Please note that this type of material is not recommended for areas with high moisture levels. It is also recommended that you do not steam clean or wet shampoo jute rugs.*
>
> *Traditionally used as carpet backing, jute is one of the finest and softest of natural floor covering materials.*
>
> *Different weights of yarn create finer or heavier textures. The fibers have a fine, silky soft luster which brings brightness and beauty to any interior. Because jute is so soft, it is ideal for bedroom floors, sitting rooms, but is not a practical material for areas of heavy wear.*
>
> ***About Sisal***
>
> *Our wool sisal rugs are appropriate for high humidity climates or high moisture areas. They discourage bacterial growth and are non-toxic and non-allergenic. Did you know that wool rugs actually purify indoor air?! Wool rugs purify indoor air, eliminating common contaminants by locking the contaminants deep in the core of the fiber, improving the indoor air quality and helping you breathe easier.*

That's a good start. This copy is definitely addressing some of her questions. But where's the comparison chart? Where do you spell out, "if you're planning on using this rug for this room, this would be a better choice." We'll take a closer look at this example in the next chapter.

Why is answering her questions so important? *The website or company that does the best job of answering her questions stands the best chance of getting her business.* She gains confidence and trust, and you build rapport with her by being resourceful and helpful. Plus, she does not have to leave your site to find the information she needs. You provide her with everything she needs to feel comfortable and confident enough to make a purchase.

How Your Salespeople Can Answer Her Questions

Your salespeople must be trained to answer her questions, not just spout the product benefits you want her to know about.

Take financial services. You are talking to a sixty-five-year-old woman who was recently widowed. She has no way to earn income. Her entire well-being depends on how much money she can save. Typical copy aimed at this woman says things like:

> *Don't let a wrong investment or improper planning set you back. Request our free report "Controlling Risk on Your Way to Retirement" to learn:*
>
> - *How different investments can affect your portfolio*
> - *The importance of finding the right asset allocation (investment mix)*
> - *About investment strategies that are available for you (such as diversification)*

Here are the questions she's actually asking:

- Will I be eating cat food when I'm eighty-five?
- What kind of cutbacks will I have to make in the way I live so my money won't run out?
- What happens if the money does run out?
- What happens if I become ill? Who's going to take care of me? Will I have enough money to be cared for at home, or will I have to go into a nursing home?
- If I die, who will take care of my pet?
- If I fall down in the house and can't get to a phone, how long will it take someone to notice?

- How can I invest the money so it will grow, but so I can't lose it all if the stock market goes to hell?
- Will I have to go back to work? How can I make money at my age?
- How can I make sure I leave money to my children without the government getting three-quarters of everything I have?
- I don't trust the man at the bank my husband used. He never included me in any of the conversations or decisions. He's done nothing but railroad me into making quick decisions and doesn't answer my questions. I want to talk to someone else. How can I go about finding a financial planner I trust? One who will look out for me? One who will take the time to talk to me without making me feel like I'm wasting his precious time?

See the difference? She's not asking about portfolios and asset allocation and diversification. She may be interested in these things as part of her education and as vehicles to provide solutions to her financial goals. You do not have to talk down to her or treat her like she can't understand (BIG mistake). But if you start off the conversation by addressing her questions, you build instant trust and credibility.

> *You're probably concerned about what's going to happen to your lifestyle, and if you'll have enough money to continue to do the things you enjoy. It's scary to feel like you don't have a way to earn income. We can talk about how much money is left, and what to do to make sure it won't run out. There are things we can do to grow your money so you can live the life you want, but still be able to sleep at night. Just because you're not working doesn't mean you don't have ways to generate income.*

Think that will resonate with her more than:

> *We specialize in wealth management, financial planning, and investment services. We'll make sure your portfolio has the correct asset allocation and diversification to protect you from unpredictable market volatility.*

Here's something to keep in mind: When answering her questions, do not be condescending. You must be genuine in your offer to help. The second she feels like you're talking down to her, she's out of there.

If you want to be her hero, you can try the old-fashioned approach:

> *It's a scary volatile world out there. You can trust me and my expertise to shield you from those dark forces and keep your money safe.*

But there's another approach:

> *There's a lot of uncertainty out there, but I'm going to educate you about what your options are. You have more power and control than you think. I'll be here to help guide you along the way.*

Think women are afraid to make their own investment decisions? Don't think they'll buy this approach? Then why is *Rich Woman: A Book on Investing for Women—Because I Hate Being Told What to Do!* by Kim Kiyosaki on the Amazon best-seller list as we write this book? (It was number seventy-three on the business and investing best seller list on October 19, 2006.)

While she may like the idea of a knight in shining armor (especially if you look like Brad Pitt in *Troy*), she may prefer to ride alongside you on her own steed.

Discovering Her Objections

Understanding her objections also goes to understanding her deeper motivations:

- She may object that "it's too expensive." But what she's really thinking is, "I don't have enough ammunition to justify the purchase of this to my boss."
- "I'm not sure this dress is really me" could mean "It's different from my usual style. Will my friends make fun of me?"

- "I really don't have time to speak at your function" could be an excuse, when she's really thinking, "I'm scared to death of public speaking."

What's the best way to handle her objections? Is it bad to bring up something negative? You don't want to put that negative thought into her head if she's not thinking about it. Is it best to ignore it? The answer is "No," you MUST address her objections. Period. Why? She's not going to take the action you want her to take if you haven't answered all of her questions, and that includes her objections.

Sean D'Souza, the mastermind behind Psychotactics.com, explains it this way: In his book, *The Brain Audit* . . . The brain acts like a conveyor belt. Imagine you go on a trip and you have seven bags. When you land at an airport, you're not walking out the exit (the conversion action) until you've gotten every one of those bags off the conveyor belt.

> *The reason why customers don't buy—It's a good idea to watch customers. Do you notice how they get a little edgy? Have you seen how they mull over paperwork? How they say they'd like to think about it? Fidget, fidget, fidget they go. Then it's mumble something under their breath time and you never see them again. Welcome. You're officially in the land of the classic conveyor belt system. You have managed to take off some of the bags in the customer's brain, and the customer is somewhat sold on your offering, but stops just short of purchasing it.*
>
> — Sean D'Souza, www.psychotactics.com

You have to answer ALL of her questions. You have to get ALL the bags off the conveyor belt, and that includes objections.

Think about how most salespeople handle objections: "You're asking the wrong question. What you should be asking is . . . ." Ouch! She's asking the *wrong question?* You've just insulted her AND avoided answering. She's not going to hear another word you say until you answer that question. It's stuck in her head, playing in a never-ending loop. Answer it up front and honestly. Otherwise, nothing you say will cause her to take the action you want her to take.

According to Sean D'Souza: "Feeling is everything. A sale can stall at this point because of lack of empathy with the customer."

There we are again: The importance of having empathy for your customer. By addressing her objection, you are *strengthening your relationship, not weakening it.*

Men have complained for ages that women are not clear in their communications. They lament that women expect them to read between the lines and understand their meaning through nuances. So how do you figure out what her objections are if she won't come out and tell you?

Once again, personas are wonderful vehicles for addressing objections. They let you understand the needs and deeper motivations of your customers and how they approach the buying process. Mine information from your call centers and your salespeople to see where customers get stuck, where the hesitations come in. Train your salespeople to ask key questions in order to zoom in on what her true feelings are.

Online Personas

In using personas online, remember that when she's on your website, she's having a conversation with you. Every click is a question she's asking. Some of those questions may convey objections.

Look at your Frequently Asked Questions section. FAQ's are FULL of objections: *"What happens if I can't retrieve me data?" "How do I know my credit card information will be kept safe?" "What if I don't like the work your designer presents? Do I still have to pay for it?" "Will my child hate me if I force him into your treatment center?"*

Don't force someone to go to your FAQ page to get critical questions answered. Instead, do it throughout your selling process, whether it's a live salesperson or on your website.

Use hyperlinks to get her to pages that address and overcome her objections. If you're worried about leaving a negative thought in someone's mind, phrase the link so the possible objection is first, then the solution is the hyperlink:

- *Worried about whether your sensitive information will be kept secure? Our state-of-the-art security program keeps your information completely safe.*

- *Many parents worry that placing a child in a treatment center will cause long-term resentment. We include the family in the healing process, allowing you to reconnect with your child.*
- *Not sure if you want to spend the full subscription fee? Sign up for a free 30- day trial to see for yourself how our services can benefit you.*

Address her objection head-on, then explain how you can overcome it. Be direct. Trying to shy away from it will make you look less than credible. And if she doesn't get that bag off her conveyor belt, she's not leaving the airport or taking whatever action you want her to take.

Conclusion

When you're building your personas, make sure you identify what questions they are asking, what their objections are, and what deeper motivations they have. Armed with that kind of insight, you can create better, more successful customer experiences. You will be much better equipped to persuade your customers to take the actions you want them to take. The secret is taking care of their needs *first*. They have to achieve their goals before you can achieve your goals.

So how do you build that customer experience? It's all about planning persuasive scenarios.

Scenarios:

Planning Pathways for Your Personas

We've talked about personas and their differing needs, motivations, and objections. But how do you plan your marketing campaign or website to accommodate these personas and their different buying processes?

You plan scenarios. You build pathways with clear starting points and ending points. These pathways include the information each persona is looking for and provide a clear way for them to accomplish their goals. Planning scenarios is a key component of Future Now Inc.'s methodology, Persuasion Architecture™. Once again, for a more in-depth look at planning scenarios and to learn more about Persuasion Architecture™ we recommend *Waiting For Your Cat to Bark.*

Let's take a high-level look at scenarios. The secret to scenarios is not only looking at the macro action, or the main action you want your persona to take, but also looking at all the micro actions she takes along the way and planning for each and every action.

Perhaps the best way to demonstrate this would be to look at a real-world scenario.

Scenario: Holly Wants to Buy a Rug Online

Holly needs to buy rugs for her new loft apartment. She wants something natural-looking, and she has heard jute carpeting is nice, not very expensive, and casual. She thinks it will match her causal country-decorating motif.

She goes to Google and types in "jute rugs."

She clicks on an organic link (below the paid links) and sees a landing page that looks something like this:

Landing pages like this are problematic because there is no clear call to action in the active window. How does Holly continue from here?

So, Holly goes back to the search engine and clicks on a paid link.

Um, OK. Which one of these is jute? Or are any of them jute? Holly does not see what she's looking for, so she goes back and clicks on another organic non-paid result. She sees a page with nothing but text in the active window.

Sisal and Jute Area Rugs

Looking for an area rug that is simple but elegant? Look no further. Our full line of sisal rugs will answer all of your needs. Not only are our rugs stylish, but we also offer them at a great discount. All of our rugs are 100% pure wool, which gives you both elegance and durability.

What is Sisal?

Sisal is a natural fiber extracted from the long leaves of sisal plants. After the leaves are crushed, the green pulp is scraped away to leave long fibers, which are then dried and prepared for weaving. Because of their unique look, sisal rugs are a great way to decorate your home or office.

Jute Rugs

Jute rugs are very elegant and durable, and they are a great way to add a touch of class and comfort to any room. We have jute rugs in all colors, shapes, sizes—even reversible rugs! We also offer a unique cotton-bound collection. These rugs are 100% pure natural jute with non-skid backing and 100% cotton binding.

What makes Jute unique?

Jute is the softest of all the natural fibers, which makes it the choice selection for areas of moderate floor traffic. Grown and harvested in Bangladesh and India, jute is known for its natural color and appearance. All of our sisal and jute rugs are available at a great discount! We value our customers, and we do our best to keep our rugs inexpensive and our prices low.

Wow, nice explanation of jute and sisal. Thank you! Holly is liking these folks already, but there are no links in the active window taking her to these jute and sisal rugs. The left hand navigation did not list them as choices either.

So, it's back to the search engine again. Holly clicks and is taken to a landing page with lots of thumbnail pictures of rugs.

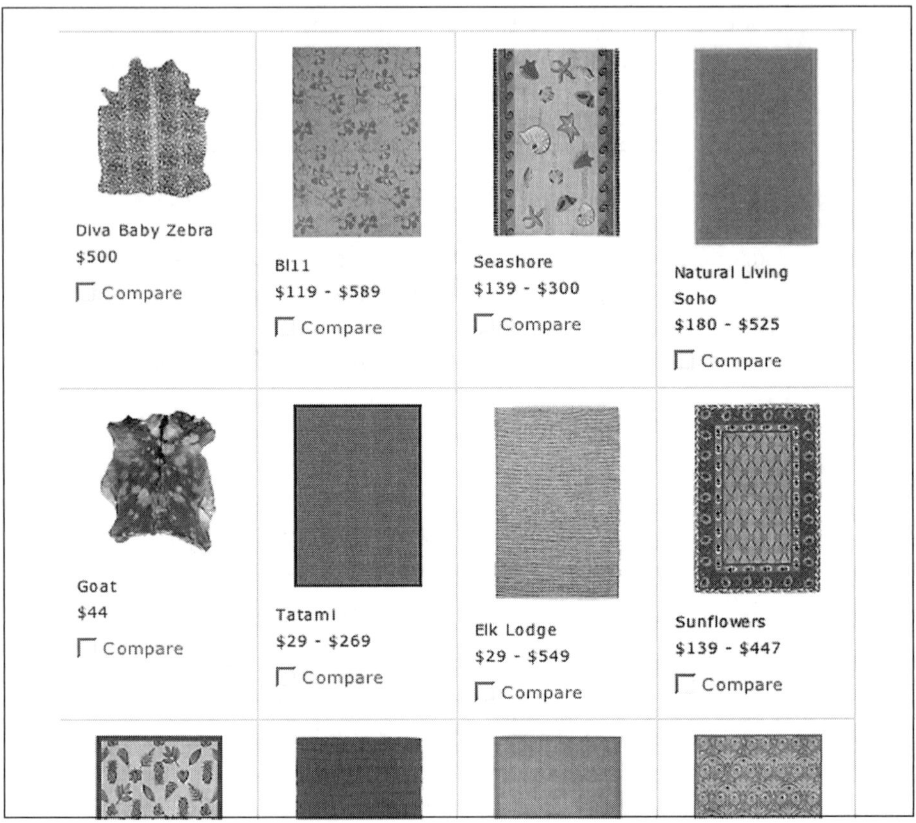

Tatami looks good so Holly clicks on that, but finds out that it is not jute; it is made of seagrass. What is seagrass? The product page gives no explanation.

Holly wants to know what the difference is between jute, sisal, and seagrass. Holly's questions are: Which one is more wear-resistant? (Lots of people will be trampling on it.) Which one is more stain-resistant? (Her friends have an inability to drink red wine without spilling.) Which one is softer? (She likes to walk around barefoot, and her Boston Terrier prefers softer rugs for napping purposes.)

So, what happens at this point? Holly has lost confidence and returns to Google to do more exploration as to what sisal, jute and seagrass are so she can determine which one is best for her needs. As so often happens, the product pages did not answer Holly's questions.

Some product pages at least start to answer questions. Like this one for a natural fiber rug.

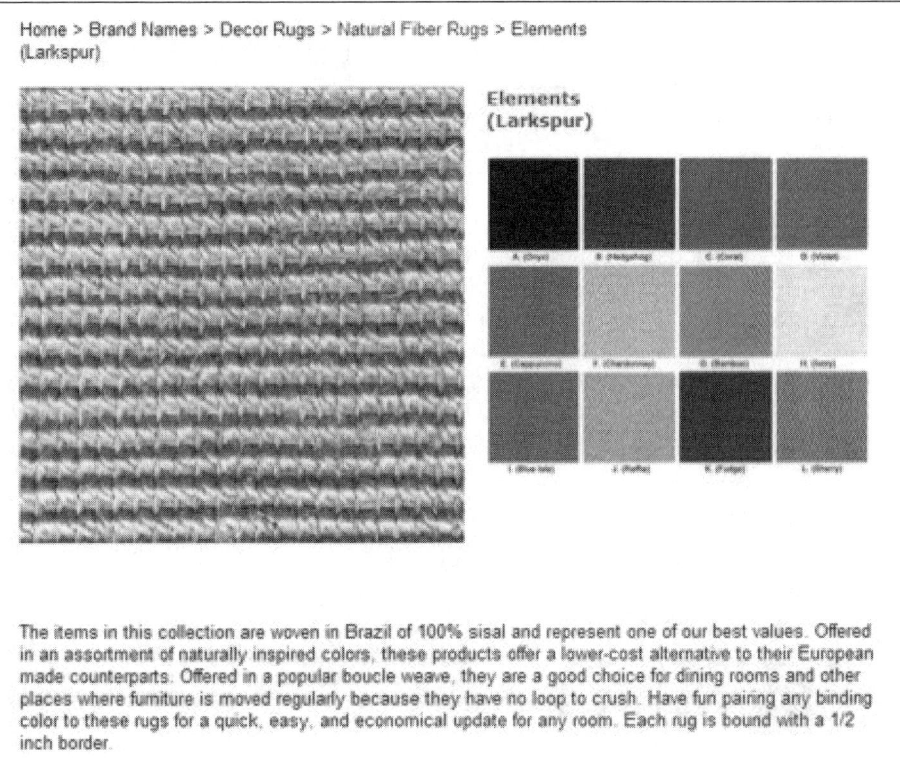

On this product page copy they at least let you know this rug is a good choice for dining rooms and why. But in the previous scenario, the rug websites did not answer Holly's questions at the point at which she was asking them. That's why planning scenarios is so important. By doing this, you'll be answering your visitors' questions, AND you'll be answering them at the all-important point at which they are asking them.

Let's look at another scenario.

Buy This CD Scenario

A music company sends Holly an e-mail touting a great new CD. They know Holly loves to buy new music.

The music company sends the following e-mail to Holly's inbox:

We've noticed that customers who have purchased Audio CDs by 4 Strings also purchased *Come With Me*. For this reason, you might like to know that *Come With Me* is now available. You can order your copy by following the link by following the link below.

Come With Me
Roger Sanchez
Price: $18.98

Holly has indeed enjoyed music by The 4 Strings, so she clicks on the indicated link. This is what she sees:

This is where the trouble begins. Holly would like to listen to samples of the music, so she scrolls down the page. The tracks of the CD are listed, but you can't click on them to listen to samples. So Holly is now forced to go to the only other choice she has to find out more about this CD, which is the customer review. Check it out:

6 of 15 people found the following review helpful:
YUK!!! What Happened?, June 27, 2006
By JBizzle "Da Fizzle Shizzle, Dizzle" (Under A Rock) - See all my reviews
I loved Sanchez's first album "First Contact", so when I heard he was finally ready to release another album, I was excited. Well, talk about a dissapointment, there wasn't one track, even remotely listenable on this album. Nothing but overblown big diva vocals over your basic lame generic house beats. I gotta ask "Roger, what happened buddy?" There were so many classic singles off "FC", and now this is the best you can come up with as a follow up? I don't know maybe some one out there will really enjoy this album. In my opinion there is not one salvagable track on this entire album, just garbage from beginning to end. Did you not listen to this before you released it dude, it's awful? I've tried to let it warm on me and play it a couple more times hoping maybe I'd enjoy it more after a couple listens... NO!!! The CD just isn't good and has absolutely no redeamable quality what so ever. Unless you're a fan of big blistering generic garbage, you might wanna skip this one, I wish I would've. What happened dude?

"Yuk!!! What Happened?" Did they even *check* to see what kind of reviews this album had when they sent out God-only-knows how many e-mails promoting this new CD? There's only one review, and it's very credible. This is obviously someone who knows what he is talking about.

Needless to say, Holly does not purchase the CD.

If the music company had planned this scenario better, they could have done a few things to increase sales. First: This is sent out to someone who has NOT bought music by this artist, but a different artist. If the scenario was "Hey, you bought this guy's music before, so check out his new CD," then it might not have been as big a deal that you could not listen to any of the tracks.

But that wasn't the scenario. The company sent this e-mail to people who had bought a CD by a different artist, making it even more important to provide a sample of the music.

Who knows what the timing was on the post of that one lone review, but perhaps they could have noticed that there was only one review, and that it was panning the CD. They might have rethought the timing. Once again, if the artist had been one Holly was already familiar with, she might not have given the review much merit if it did not coincide with her own experience. But she wasn't familiar with this artist, which made her more susceptible to this reviewer's opinion.

By now you're getting a sense of the importance of planning scenarios for your customers. You must anticipate your customers' needs. Plan your customer experience so every step of the way, she can get her questions answered and has access to links that propel her forward on her pathway. She should never hit a page where she has to stop and think: *Where do I go next*?

For a more in-depth look at planning scenarios for your personas, we suggest reading *Waiting For Your Cat To Bark* by Bryan and Jeffrey Eisenberg.

Conclusion

Planning scenarios is key to all your marketing efforts, not just your website. From your television ads, to your radio ads, to your PPC campaigns, to your e-mail campaigns, to your in-store experience, *look at your messaging and what each next step entails*. Don't look at your efforts separately; look at how your customers move from one marketing medium to the next. If your television commercial is touting a special promotion and includes your website URL, make darn sure your home page includes information about that promotion. Coordinating these multi-channel efforts is essential to your success.

Look at who your personas are and plan scenarios so they can easily get their needs met and accomplish their goals. By planning these scenarios, you can eliminate many of the problems and disconnects your customers might otherwise experience when trying to do business with you. In the web world, we call that "increasing conversions." In your world it's called "increasing sales." Ka-ching!

By now you may be thinking, *I see the value in building personas and scenarios, but how do I gather the information I need to do that? How do I get that kind of insight into my customers?*

We've got some suggestions on that.

PART V

The Inside-Out of Your Customers . . . and *Your Business*

13

Third Wave Research:

Effective Methods for Understanding Women from the Inside Out

You've been brought in for questioning when suddenly it occurs to you that offering to help might have been a bad idea.

It's a scene from a second-rate detective film. You're in a confined, airless room with bright, harsh lights that make you squint and wonder to yourself what time it really is outside. Except for a mirror, the walls are bare. The only pieces of furniture are several chairs strategically placed around a small table, the top worn smooth from hours of nervous, drumming fingers.

The room is filled with strangers and the sense of unease is palpable. For two hours, the interrogator has been pumping you for information, working hard to coerce you into giving up the goods. "Just tell us the truth," the interrogator keeps coaxing, "just tell us what we want to hear." But you don't *know* what they want to hear. By now, in fact, you don't even know how you ended up in this dead-end chamber of horrors. You realize your only means of escape will be to say whatever it takes to make them happy, even if it means lying.

We've all seen Hollywood's cliché of the interrogation room, with a tough, no-nonsense suit questioning the witness until he squeals. If it all sounds eerily familiar, however, perhaps that's because it's also the description of a typical *focus group session.*

In today's world, how are you conducting consumer research? Do you look to typical quantitative demographics like zip codes, age, and income to help you target your customer base? Are you still relying on traditional methods like focus groups to compile what you deem to be qualitative data? If you are, that is (as a young friend of ours would say) just *so twentieth century*.

It's easy to get sucked into a whirlpool of numbers when you're trying to understand who your customer is. You've been taught to look at how old she is, what part of town she lives in, and how much money she makes per year. When you're planning your advertising strategy, media outlets all seem to magically reach the exact demographic you are looking for. They are notorious for shooting off impressive figures when trying to get you to advertise in their publication or on their radio or television station.

You've got the numbers, but this really doesn't tell you who she is *inside*, does it? So, you take the next logical step in getting to know her, an in-store survey. But beware the trap this sets, for you'll be interviewing a fish out of water. In recent years, research data compiled through woman-on-the-street surveys has proven to be more and more unreliable. When it comes to surveys, subjects often feel uncomfortable in a location outside their own personal environment. Stop a woman in a mall, ask her how many pairs of designer shoes she has in her closet, and the answer could be off by as many as twenty. Question her about the food she feeds her kids and she may tell a little white lie, not wanting to admit, perhaps even to herself, the truth about all the hot dogs and Spaghettios her kids consume.

OK, you say, let's dig deeper. Let's try some focus groups. Surely *this* will tell you all about her, right?

Wrong.

In a traditional focus-group situation, women who don't know one another are thrown together into a sterile corporate-type boardroom and asked for their opinions on specific products or services. And here's where the problems start.

Depending on the women's personalities, they're going to react in different ways. Some will clam up. They're introverted by nature and will offer little of what's going on inside their head. Others will quickly become the alpha of the group, dominating the discussion by throwing opinions around the room like a two-ton medicine ball. Those left in the middle often feel compelled to follow the leader, whether or not they agree. The result ends up being data infected by the most vocal people in the room, or sometimes by marketing executives themselves (depending on internal pressures to "come up with the right answer").

The pressure-cooker atmosphere of a group of strangers in an unfamiliar setting being asked questions skewed to obtain answers favorable toward a product is often a dangerous (if not deadly) concoction. Over the years, countless products that should never have been introduced made it to market, and vice versa. Ideas that rated highly among focus groups often failed miserably in the real world.

Third Wave Research

Recently, companies like Yahoo!, Pepsi, and Best Buy have begun to realize that methods they undertook to mine for information in the past were often unproductive and inefficient. Today, they are taking advantage of major advancements in science, technology, and human behavior to study consumers in ways that are more natural and provide greater insight into what a customer wants.

Internet Research Panels

Research services like Invoke Solutions and Greenfield Online are providing businesses with a way to connect with customers at the computer keyboard. They gather groups of consumers to participate on panels via instant-messaging services. In the comfort of their own individual spaces, participants feel more at ease to answer honestly (and anonymously). Important, effective data also can be compiled within hours rather than over weeks or months.

When Pepsi was looking for Gen-Xers' opinions on mineral water, it turned to Invoke for help. Using the online IM panel system, it was easy to see that participants were highly interested in water with an elevated mineral content. Great news, but that also would mean upping the sugar content to make it taste better, something consumers *didn't* want. Nearly overnight, Pepsi had the answer it needed. "Conclusions that could take three to four months to sort out through focus groups . . . get settled in a few hours," says David Rubinstein of Invoke in an interview for *BusinessWeek (November 5, 2005).*

Immersion Groups and Ethnography

"Marketing anthropology" is more and more prevalent in present-day research. Instead of bringing the customer to them, some companies are going directly to the customer. While research groups have long studied shopping behavior in places like malls, a few are now taking the next step, observing consumer behavior by immersing researchers into the home, either live or remotely by camera. It's their goal to interact directly with customers to study how they live and explore what specific individual needs are going unfulfilled.

Kimberly-Clark, the maker of Huggies diapers, experienced recent success in working to understand how mothers change diapers and bathe babies. After placing a small headset camera atop a mother's head, Kimberly-Clark researchers then sat back and began to watch mothers go about their daily routines. In traditional focus groups, mothers had indicated they mainly used changing tables; now researchers discovered that mothers actually change diapers just about anywhere there's an open space—floors, sofas, even the tops of washing machines. This means a constant struggle with packaging that requires two hands. By using the information from this immersion method of research, engineers were able to redesign the packaging of their products for easy use with one hand. The result? A resurgence in the popularity of the Huggies diaper brand.

Research Tools You Can Use

Is the use of Internet panels, ethnography, and immersion effective? Absolutely. But not every business has the resources or budget to invest in research of this magnitude. There are, however, several things you can do that will provide solid, powerful information to help develop your personas. Using some basic but comprehensive methods, you'll gain a greater understanding of your customers' needs and how your business fits into the solution.

As an added bonus, Persuasion Architecture™ based personas can also be a valuable research tool. Once you plan scenarios for your personas, you can test to see what your customers actually do and if they follow those scenarios. You can gather very valuable information from their behavior. Are they doing what you predicted they would do? If not, why not? They are giving you feedback on whether or not your hypotheses about them are correct. With this feedback, you can now optimize your scenarios, providing the best possible customer experience.

Mini Immersion Projects

Even though you may not have the resources to send a team into the field to observe consumers in their homes, you can still get information from people that helps you learn more about their everyday lives. One way is to have participants do the research for you. Let's say you sell closet organization systems. Hold a "Biggest Closet Disaster" contest and have people send in videos or photos with essays about why their (or their mother's or girlfriend's) closet should be crowned the biggest disaster, then offer the winner a free closet makeover. You'll not only create great word-of-mouth (and probably some public relations, as well), but you'll gain vast amounts of information on how people use their closets, what their priorities are, and what individual needs are going unfulfilled—needs that your competitors haven't even thought about. Fertile ground for future advertising copy!

A Board of Customer Evangelists

In their book *Creating Customer Evangelists*, authors Jackie Huba and Ben McConnell, champion companies of all sizes that tap into the love customers have for their brand. They recommend the creation of an ad hoc evangelist board, half a dozen or so of your most loyal customers, who would love to get together a couple times a year for dinner and let you pick their brains. Do you want honest feedback about what you're doing right and wrong? These customers will tell you. Find out how they're using your product and service. Are they missing something you assumed they knew how to do? Are they utilizing what you sell in ways you never dreamed, ways that should be shared with others? A solid board of committed customers (with no other investment in your business) will provide you with more marketing information than a dozen demographic studies or focus groups.

Tapping Into Online Communities

One effective way of gathering consumer perspective is to seek out and connect with already-existing online communities that can offer perspectives directly related to your product or service. Companies like Hewlett-Packard, Kraft, and Glaxo-SmithKline have tapped into these Internet villages, and have gained much deeper consumer insight than from ordinary focus groups. Glaxo, conducting research for the upcoming release of a weight-loss pill, recently found itself in deep conversation with a group of participants from an online weight-loss community. Participants offered advice, opinions, objections, and personal stories that will affect everything from advertising to packaging. "They have done an incredible job of reaching out into the community and giving us all hope that someone out there cares about us and we are not alone in our struggle to lose weight," proclaimed one participant in an article for *BusinessWeek (September 4, 2006).*

Conversation Groups

Rather than study a group's reaction to a specific product or service, a few smart businesses are getting to know their customer "inside out," from the perspective of human behavior.

In our work with clients, we are often hired to design "conversation sessions," where groups of four to six friends meet in a host home to discuss general views on life. These "girl parties" provide information that helps companies understand at what stage of life the participants find themselves.

Sitting with a glass of wine, women discuss their dreams, worries, and thoughts about the future. These women are friends (sometimes for as long as forty or fifty years) and feel comfortable with the group. They encourage one another but also know one another so well that they don't hesitate to call "bull-hooey" on a statement they think is false or out of character.

As a conversation group settles into a groove, small pieces of "information gold" start bubbling to the surface. You begin to hear what participants really think about life *and* what's missing. You discover what their needs are, and with the right questions from a strong moderator, you begin to see how your product or service can fill that need.

Suddenly, it clicks in: You know where to place these women on Maslow's hierarchy, and it becomes clear what level of need you should be focusing on. A few participants will fall above or below the core level that matches what your business offers, but that's OK. The important thing is to focus on what you can consistently deliver to the group that needs you most. You'll also have learned what you need to do in the future, when you find yourself at the point of "kicking it up a notch" on Maslow's hierarchy, to serve a higher level of need than that of your competitors.

Because conversation groups focus more on understanding a woman's entire life, you get a better understanding of her deeper motivations. The smaller size of these groups, the comfortable setting, and the fact that the women know each other provides an intimacy and trust you cannot achieve in traditional focus groups. That intimacy and trust leads to more revealing information.

Best Buy Gains a New Perspective

One of Michele's clients is consumer electronics giant Best Buy. Founded in 1966, under the name Sound of Music, Best Buy is now the nation's largest retailer of consumer electronics, with more than seven hundred stores in the United States.

Acknowledging the fact that the customer playing field has changed dramatically during the last few years, the consumer research department at Best Buy headquarters has been hard at work delving into what really makes customers tick. The researchers had experienced some success with the creation of a customer profile they named "Jill" (think Soccer Mom), but they realized they needed to go deeper into the individual needs of different female consumers to find out exactly how women approach the technology of today's world.

In a series of conversation group sessions that Michele created and moderated, Best Buy executives were allowed access into consumers' homes, listening in as women of different ages and lifestyles talked about their lives. Single, married, children, no children, college age or Baby Boomers—the overlap of needs, values, and views on technology was an eye-opener for Best Buy.

An example of quotes from the Baby Boomer group revealed a very different way of thinking about life than expressed by the same age group twenty years earlier:

> *"There was a phase in my life where it was 'protecting your family' . . . making sure that my daughter had Guess jeans—making sure that my son had his Air Jordan tennis shoes. Making sure that the*

material things were there. The shift has gone from material to non-material things. It's more spiritual but it's not a structured, religious-type spirituality—it's bigger than that."

—Sue

"I'm afraid of retirement and what it has to offer me. My father retired at an early age and I watched him dwindle because he didn't have the job, he didn't have the contacts. He moved from New York down to Florida, he was away from all his really good friends, and his source of strength. Before he got really sick he said to me in a conversation that one of the biggest mistakes he made was retiring too early. And it's always kinda stuck in my mind. I mean just cuz you turn sixty-five you're turning off a very, very important part of your life. As much as people don't want to admit it, our jobs define us as people . . . our family does, our homes do, but I think a job is probably the biggest part of that."

—Regina

"I learned just recently that the Baby Boomers feel like they're not going to die. They're just going to go on and on . . . at a meeting I was at, we were told, "You have a responsibility to die." You've gotta get out of the way for the other generations coming through, and that's really hard for us. We kinda laugh about it and say "Yeah, we know we have to," but I don't think we really believe it. We don't feel old . . . we've taken care of ourselves . . . when you think about what our grandparents were like at our ages, oh my gosh, they were ancient!"

—Lauree

"When I go to a store, and I'm looking to buy something technological—a camera, iPod, whatever . . . I wanna see everything. I want to see the basic product and I want to see all of its accessories together. I don't want to have to go over to the earphone department, I don't want to have to go over to the iPod department, I don't want to have to go to the hard drive department, and it may just be an aisle away. I want them all together and of the same compatibility and like to make it very simple. It's interesting because men, at least my husband, find it very

> *frustrating to have it prepared like I want it. He would rather go to the various aisles for the specifics, because he's comparing one set of earphones against another, one hard drive against the other. But if I knew there were a hard drive and here's the various screens or flat screens, if I'm looking for flat screens, close by in proximity, that are compatible, that's where I would stay. I'm looking for one-stop shopping."*
>
> —*Carol*

"We found we needed to change our perspective on women and technology," says Tara Hutchinson, former senior manager of consumer research at Best Buy. "When we used the word technology, their eyes glazed over and they were very anti-tech. But when we changed it around and started talking about what technology does for their individual worlds, they came alive. They love technology, they just use a different language than has been traditionally used in consumer electronics. With female consumers, we have to move away from 'high-tech' and toward 'high touch.'"

Using information gathered during the conversation sessions and in-store group shopping excursions, Best Buy was able to build the foundation for several personas, each of which has its own needs and desires. It remains to be seen how successful Best Buy will be in integrating these personas into its advertising, website and sales training, but they are already light-years ahead of their competitors when it comes to getting to know what the female consumer is looking for.

Online Surveys

The beauty of online surveys is they are fast, easy, and cheap. The bad news is, it's tough to get people to participate. And, despite the anonymity of the web, their answers are not always completely truthful. But there are things you can do to increase response rates and create carefully worded questions that will actually give you useful answers and insight.

How do you address the fact that people are not always 100 percent truthful in their answers? We all love to pretend we're people we're not. One of Holly's fondest memories of her sister was the time she put on her Cinderella costume and refused to take it off for two days (her sister was thirty-two at the time). We all want to portray positive images of ourselves. The beauty of online surveys is, there is an element of anonymity. But sometimes we genuinely aren't aware of our shortcomings.

As much as she says "I want you to understand me" she may not always tell you the truth about herself. She's not purposefully lying, but the image of ourselves we want to project to the world and who we really are, often may not be the same thing.

HOLLY: I was talking to a friend who had a financial/investment services client.

The client offered two types of investment advice and services. One service was geared toward value investors, those who are risk averse and comfortable with slower growth, more of a buy and hold strategy. The other service was designed for an investor who is much more aggressive. This investor wants the hot stocks, triple digit returns, and quick turnarounds. The client believed the audience was evenly split. But when the client did an online survey, the vast majority of visitors classified themselves as value investors. So the company was considering changing the content on the site to speak more to this less aggressive investor.

When my friend told me about the online survey, I gave her a highly professional technical analysis:

"It's crap."

OF COURSE visitors filling out the online survey were going to say they were disciplined value investors. OF COURSE they think of themselves as smart long-term planners happy with steady growth. Who's going to willingly raise their hand and say "Not me—I chase every high flying stock opportunity with the wild abandon of a giddy schoolgirl in hope of bagging the next triple digit winner." But you only have to look at the plethora of websites and trading services that make megabucks with headlines like "this stock is poised to rocket up 200 percent in the next thirty days."

I consider myself a low-risk value investor. But I'm embarrassed to tell you how much money I've lost trying to find the next eBay or Qualcomm. I finally had to hire a financial advisor whose job it is to *specifically* talk me out of bad stock ideas. "But Pete—the newsletter said this trial drug could end childhood disease, save the rainforest, and cure cancer! But if I don't get in now, I could miss out on billions of dollars!!" He gently points out that the technical chart looks awful, the company has no track record of ever having produced anything, and it's located in Botswana.

I truly want to be, and describes myself as, a value investor. That's what I'll tell you in a survey. But am I still tempted by those promises of big returns and getting in on the next Google or high flying IPO? Am I interested in aggressive investing? Yes. Even though I try to avoid it, I'm still turned on by aggressive investing copy and offers.

So how do you handle this in your surveys? **Be very careful how you phrase your questions.** Try to keep any sort of judgment out of your verbiage. We're all easily influenced and swayed by suggestive language. The question "How fast were the cars going when they crashed?" will get higher mph answers than "At what speed were the cars traveling when the accident occurred?"

If you're asking people to divulge information that may be less than flattering, give them permission to be truthful. Instead of "Do you eat healthy or unhealthy snacks?" You might rephrase it "When you feel the urge to snack, do you choose healthy alternatives, or sometimes is a candy bar or sweet the only thing that really does it for you?" The shift in language is subtle, but the verbiage is softer, less accusing.

Guidelines for creating online surveys:

1. Keep them as short as possible. The longer the survey is, the fewer people will fill it out.
2. Let them know ahead of time approximately how long it will take. A more exact time frame works better than a vague time frame. "Three minutes" is stronger than "not very long."
3. Start out with easier questions first. Put more personal questions toward the end.
4. Don't use influencing language. Be very careful how you word your questions. Instead of "Is there anything offensive about this name?" you could ask, "How do you feel about this name—what images come to mind?"
5. When possible, use open-ended questions where you can get an actual written answer. This provides enormous insight into what

people are really thinking and is a goldmine for keywords and copy ideas. (The trade-off is it requires more time and thinking. Multiple-choice answers are much easier and more likely to be filled out, so weigh the pros and cons of each option.)

6. Tell them why you are doing the survey and what you're doing with the information. Women love to give their opinion, but even more importantly, they love to be heard. Let them know you heard their suggestions, opinions, or show them how you used their information in a positive way.
7. Three words—privacy, privacy, privacy. Let them know clearly and up front who will be seeing their information and whom it will be shared with.
8. Be careful in your choice of rewards. Yes, it's really nice to be rewarded for your time. Incentives can increase participation. But you will get the best answers from women who feel you truly value their opinion and will take action based on their feedback. If you do offer a reward, try to tie it into your brand. Instead of a chance at a vacation, perhaps offer her 10 percent off her next purchase at your store.

Use these guidelines for creating online surveys and enjoy the valuable data they generate. But pay close attention to how you *interpret* this data. If you get answers that surprise you, do more digging to find out what's really going on. If you're asking people to divulge information that may not portray them in a positive light, be extra careful how you read the results.

Blog Comments

If you have a company blog, you can use it to reach out and start a conversation with your customers. You have a choice with your blog of whether or not to enable reader comments. We always recommend you allow readers to comment. It's a great way to have interaction with and get direct feedback from your customers. Plus, if there's a specific subject you want feedback on, write a post and ask for comments. "We're updating our software. Which of these features would you most like to see?"

Beware—you will get negative comments. Sometimes it's tough to stomach them, but they often provide valuable insight. Yes, if someone has a potty mouth or is completely out of line, you can delete the negative comment. But we urge you to leave them up.

Get creative. There are all sorts of ways you can use your blog to gain information on your customers. Take Stonyfield Farm's Bovine Bugle blog. (Say that three times fast.) They have a "Got a question for farmer Jonathan" feature that creates a unique chance for interaction. Start the conversation and get ready to listen.

Discussion Forums and Consumer Feedback Sites

Discussion forums and consumer feedback sites are great places to do three things:

- See what people are saying about your products.
- See what people are saying about your competition.
- See how your customers describe their problems/needs/solutions.

If you're a baby food manufacturer, visit sites where new moms congregate. See how they describe their struggles. See what's important to them, what annoys them. Listen to the language they use to describe their situation. If you're selling retirement financial planning, mine sites like www.aarp.org for information about your audience. Epinions.com and planetfeedback.com are just two examples of customer review sites that will give you all sorts of information about how customers rate you and your competitors. The Internet provides a vast wealth of information that's just a search engine away.

Web Analytics

The wonderful thing about the Internet is, you can measure everything. The problem with the Internet is, you can measure everything. With all the sophisticated web analytics programs, you can measure every click on your website. But many marketers are overwhelmed by all this data. How do you know which numbers matter the most? How can you use this knowledge to gain insight into your customers?

Good analytics and some help understanding them can go a long way toward gaining insight into what visitors are doing on your site. What these numbers don't tell you is *why* visitors are doing what they're doing. Once again, this is where persona scenarios can be very helpful. They will give you context to understand not only what your visitors are doing, but why they are doing it.

Even without these persona scenarios, you can gauge some sort of idea as to what experience your visitors are having with your website by conversion rate—in other words, how many visitors do you have and how many actually take the action you want them to take. Note that buying your product is not the only action you want your visitors to take. Signing up for a newsletter, filling out a form, forwarding information to a friend, downloading a PDF, or even just visiting pages with important information about your company or product are all conversions you want to measure.

Uncovery—Asking the Right Questions

When conducting research to learn more about the personas we're going to create, we spend a great deal of time on "uncovery." Uncovery is term Future Now Inc. uses to describe the process of going beneath the superficial mask we all wear, digging deeper to get solid, powerful information on needs and characteristics. One of the most important parts of uncovery is knowing what questions to ask. Which questions will give you the best insight into how your customers really think, feel, and buy? Which questions will help you get past their surface needs to their deeper motivations? Which questions will help you draw out their true objections?

Here's one hint: **You have to understand the context of her whole life.** Michele always starts her girl groups by having the participants focus on two questions. The women create collages based around these two questions. These questions start the conversation by getting right to what really matters to these women. What are they really thinking and feeling? What's most important in their lives?

Here's another hint: **Really good uncovery is not linear**. Sometimes you just have to have a nose for the scent of truly relevant information and follow that scent trail where it goes. Following a strict script simply doesn't work. We use a set of questions as a guideline, but we view it as a "web" rather than a linear process. We do our best to get all those questions answered, but invariably the best information comes out when you veer down a different track. Someone makes an offhand comment, your inner beagle detects a scent, goes . . . "arroooooo" and off you go.

One final hint: **Certain personality types are better at uncovery**. In the world of the Myers-Briggs personality type testing, it's easy to discover the individual strengths and internal preferences of people. When it comes to uncovery, NF's or "Intutitive Feelers" tend to be natural uncovery experts. Part of that is the N or the intuitive. Someone says something and you just intuitively know you're on to something. The F means you are a feeler. The F's are very good empathizers. They are able to put themselves into someone else's shoes, see the world through that person's eyes, and understand that person's point of view, even if it is really different from their own. Find yourself a strong NF (if you're not one yourself), and you'll have an excellent uncovery detective.

If you're getting customer insight from a client or business owner, there's an incredibly effective question that will give you wonderful insight. We always ask: "What questions are your customers asking?" This always leads to important information. But we follow that up with, "What questions *should* your customers be asking?" This often leads to important information the company has that their customers don't necessarily know about.

Another question you should always ask is, "which means?" If you really want to dig to the heart of the matter, keep asking "which means?" Holly did an interview with a couple who had just bought a house at a subdivision. She was trying to find out why they chose this subdivision instead of one of the many other similar properties in the area. Here's how it went . . .

"What was it about this subdivision or house that made you want to live here?"
"Well, it's close to where Jim works."
"So are five other subdivisions. Why this one?"
"We were able to get a special financing offer from the builder."
"Which means?"

"We were able to get more house for our money."

"Which means?"

"Instead of a three bedroom, we could afford a four bedroom. This way each of the kids can have their own room, AND Jim can have a place for a home office. Though I may fight him for it. I'd love to have a home gym."

This insight led to an advertising campaign with a couple fighting about what they would do with the extra room they could afford because they bought a home in this particular subdivision. Asking "which means . . ." uncovered the heart of the story and gave the client a marketing message that resonated with their perspective customers.

Conclusion

Researching your customer and what she really wants can be hard work, but is worth every bit of time and energy you put into it because the results tell you who she really is and what she wants from you. You will be surprised at many of the answers you get from women but if you're willing to let go of any preconceived notions, you will experience customer enlightenment. Dig deep, ask lots of questions, and ask good questions. Put on your NF hat and follow your intuition. Remove all judgment, be empathetic, and get to know her as a whole person. The insight will be well worth it.

Once you finish uncovery with your customers, you'll need to do some uncovery on yourself. Your company's values, motivations, and communication style are just as important as those of your customers.

14

Finding Your Voice:

Connecting With Her Deeper Motivations Through Authenticity and Language

HOLLY: Can you lose a sale in two words? Yes, you can. What two words could be so horrible that they'd lose a sale from a willing, qualified prospect?

"Dear Sir."

That's all it took. I was not happy with my current lawn irrigation company and was actively looking for another company to replace them. And there in my mailbox one morning was a letter from another irrigation company. I opened it eagerly because I thought: Hah! They're marketing in this neighborhood; I've heard of them; maybe they're even offering a special! I was a marketer's dream, familiar with the brand, in a high state of need, and ready to act now. Then that letter spoke two words to me . . .

"Dear Sir."

That was it. I was gone. I didn't even read the rest of the letter. I balled it up and into the trash it went. Shoot . . . into the trash it went. Damn small trash can opening . . . into the trash it went. There.

My neighborhood is littered with single people, retired people, and families, many with stay-at-home moms and a few single moms. For any of these families where the woman was the decision maker, or there was no male at all, that letter probably ended up in the same place mine did. Why? Those opening words told me one thing: This is a company run by good-old boys (there are a lot of them where I live). They want to deal with "the man of the house." They don't want to waste their time with "little ladies" like me.

Now, that may have been a completely false impression, but all that matters in this case is customer perception. At the end of the day, it is not what you say, but what your customers hear that matters.

Beware the incredible power of words and their meaning in your communication. What you say and how you say it is the difference between a sale and a rim shot into the trash.

To Thine Own Self Be True

There's something every woman has, but we'll bet you've never seen it. She doesn't parade it around in public. But it's there at her fingertips 24/7. It's something you'd better be aware of, because she uses it to guide her in every single purchasing decision she makes.

What is it? We'll give you a hint. It's shaped like a cow patty and makes an electronic buzzing noise when set off. Yup. We're talking about her bullshit detector.

With four times as many connections between the two hemispheres of the brain, a woman not only processes information at a supersonic rate, she also takes in more of the big picture. When it comes to making decisions, a woman compresses a barrage of incoming signals into manageable form, absorbing them through the filter of emotional memory, experience, and intuition.

In other words, her BS detector is in overdrive.

If something doesn't fit or seems forced or inauthentic, she's going to pick up on it. She may not know exactly what's wrong. It may only be a slight hesitation, a feeling of apprehension she can't place. But it's going to be enough to stop her from taking the action you want her to take.

Many businesses talk too much about "understanding a woman's unique needs." When you use the wrong language or you talk more than show, her BS detector is going to go off. If you really understand her, *show her*. Otherwise, she'll feel patronized.

Be Who You Are, Boldly

At the heart of every successful marketing to women campaign lies the commitment to being authentic, the true essence of who you really are. This is the foundation for all of your marketing and advertising. You must know what your real message is before you ever start thinking of creative ways to deliver it.

When it comes to authenticity, a woman notices everything: Your advertising, merchandise, website, employees, retail stores, lighting, how clean the bathrooms are, how your employees dress, what they say to her, how her purchase is shipped, the box it's shipped in, *and* the packing materials. If you say you "understand women," but your product is stacked high on a shelf she has no hope of reaching, your bathrooms aren't clean, your employees don't say "thank you," and her purchase arrives in a plain brown box stuffed with newspaper, that cow patty is going to start buzzing.

Generations of marketing overdose means that today's female consumers have a naturally heightened sensitivity to hard sell and coverup. It's also easier to change the channel, switch the station, pick up another magazine, or surf to another website. With all of the competition and clutter, not to mention a BS detector that regularly registers in the red, how can your business make an impact on a woman's life?

The first principle of marketing to women, both offline and online, is "To thine own self be true." You will begin to plant your brand in the mind of a woman only when it has proven its *authenticity* and *transparency.*

Authenticity—Straight From the Heart

Forget the hype and start thinking about the heart—*your* heart. What motivations drive you forward each day? How do your passions fit in with her passions? What do you do to make a difference in her daily life? Figure out what that is and you'll have the heart of your own personal message.

Differentiation is rooted in the personal core values that genuinely reflect the beliefs of a business, those characteristics that, if challenged, you would fight for to the bitter end. Do you believe in truth? Kindness? Which is more important to you, honesty or loyalty? Are you bound by love for others? What is first and foremost in your mind, being competitive or having integrity? Or is it a combination of both?

Before planning any marketing strategy, you must take time to explore and determine the list of values that are the very essence of your business. When that essence lives and breathes through every customer touch point on a consistent basis, your business automatically resonates with those women who share your core ideals.

Let's say, for example, you've chosen caring for others as one of your central values. Set advertising aside for the moment and ask yourself if you have really given thought to how to convey that caring in the myriad ways a customer comes in contact with you. If you're in retail, have you thought about how wide your aisles are? Is there room for a wheelchair or a stroller? Is your shopping bag designed to remind the customer how special she is? Perhaps you run your service-oriented business out of an office. Who answers the phone? How long are people left on hold? Is your website an easy-to-use reference for information she needs?

Bryan Eisenberg, co-author of the best-selling book *Waiting for Your Cat to Bark*, recently shared a personal customer experience with MaxJet, the all-business-class airline:

> Several months ago I decided I was going to fly the new, all business class airline from JFK, MaxJet, to get to London for my buddy, Jim Sterne's, Emetrics seminar. It was a fabulous experience and I told several people they needed to try it out.
>
> With all the chaos with the airlines this past week [the uncovery of a bomb plot in London], MaxJet's CEO, Gary R. Rogliano, sent out an e-mail which just about guaranteed my next trip in November will be aboard his caring airline. The text of the e-mail is below:
>
> *Dear Friend:*
>
> *The MAXjet Family is committed to getting you where you need to be, while keeping your security and safety utmost in our minds. We have*

continued to operate all of our flights as close to schedule as possible, due in large part, to the efficiency of flying into and out of London Stansted Airport.

Our primary focus right now is to maintain the safety and security of our customers, crew members, and all others involved. To that end, I want to reassure you that we are following all security directives to maximize the safety and security of our airline.

Understandably, some of you may choose to change your travel plans because of the security incident that arose this week. I've asked our excellent Customer Service, Reservations, and Airport Services teams to allow a one-time waiver for change fees and add collects for you, for changes made prior to 31 October 2006. There's more information listed on www.maxjet.com. Some flights for instance, may require authorization from Customer Care, due to availability.

Know that we are doing everything possible to keep you safe, get you to your destination as close to schedule as possible, and provide you with the best possible customer service. If you need more information, we have posted the restrictions on www.maxjet.com.

We're here to serve you and provide you safe and comfortable passage on your trip.

Warmest regards,
Gary

Gary R. Rogliano
CEO
MAXjet Airways, Inc.

What messages are you sending to your customers that show you really care about their lives, not just your business?

Bryan is right: There is no such thing as talking about authenticity, only being authentic. It's time to walk the talk: Presenting a real, memorable experience for your customer on a consistent basis is the foundation for brand loyalty.

Inner Spirit Photography: The Power of Authenticity

The first time you meet Mark Laurie, you'd probably never guess he's one of the world's preeminent portrait photographers. A down-to-earth, affable fellow with kind eyes and an easy smile, this Calgary-based photo artist has won countless awards and commendations; two of his portraits were chosen by NASA to be included in the Voyager III space capsule. Mark and his wife, Jan, have worked side by side for more than twenty-five years, capturing stunning portraits of more than four thousand women. What makes this all the more interesting is that Mark's area of expertise is intimate portraiture, art photographs of women that include lingerie, boudoir, and nude poses.

With more than four thousand women knocking on Mark and Jan's door, they must be doing something right. Between the two of them, they have an innate sense of human behavior and creativity that immediately makes clients feel comfortable in an otherwise nerve-racking situation. But part of their success can also be attributed to smart marketing. After researching shifts in society and trends toward "authenticity" in marketing, Mark recently realized he needed to make some changes to his marketing strategy and language. No matter how good you are, the "intimate photography" industry unfortunately carries with it a dark, seedy stigma of sleaze, and Mark knows he's fighting an uphill battle.

Mark had been advertising on Calgary radio for about a year when he began to reevaluate his strategy. He knew he was on target with a fifty-two-week campaign that established him as a presence in Calgary. But growth wasn't occurring as rapidly as predicted. What needed to be changed? *The language that was used to connect with women.*

Mark determined that in order to rise above the stereotype of average boudoir photographers and have a chance at projecting his core belief that "every woman is beautiful," he needed to let clients tell their own stories. He spent several weeks with dozens of willing clients, audio- and videotaping their stories, capturing their own personal experiences through the art of conversation. Edited into fifteen-second clips, the sound bites were then incorporated into thirty-second radio ads with a book-ended announcement by a male voice-over:

> ANNCR: "Lisa talks about meeting world-renowned photo artist Mark Laurie for the first time."
>
> LISA: "We just sat down and talked about different poses I could do, and what my passions were for photography, and what I wanted to look like, and Mark was like *in tune with me the whole time*! So it's like 'Sign me up! I wanna do some photographs!"
>
> ANNCR: "Experience the energy and artistry of Mark Laurie at Inner Spirit Photography . . . portraits that reflect the true you. On the web at inner-spirit-photo.com."

One ad addressed the safety and security issue by talking about "bringing a friend":

> ANNCR: "Angelique talks about sharing her Inner Spirit experience with a friend."
>
> ANGELIQUE: "I had a friend with me that day, because if you're really shy, you can always bring a friend. And she did some stuff that gave me ideas and I did some stuff that gave her ideas. And then, believe it or not, we did some stuff together, which our husbands thought was a lot of fun. And yes, I am married . . ."
>
> ANNCR: "Create beautiful, lasting memories with a portrait by award-winning photo artist Mark Laurie. By yourself or with friends—it's an experience you'll never forget! On the web at inner-spirit-photo.com."

Mark even recorded husbands and boyfriends, talking about receiving an Inner Spirit portrait as a gift.

ANNCR: "Dale talks about his girlfriend's Inner Spirit portrait experience."

DALE: "Each time we get a new photo (from the "monthly photo" collection), you get that same feeling . . . that excitement, because you know that date is coming up when you're going to get another photograph and you're not sure which one it is, with the package that we chose. It's pretty exciting!"

ANNCR: "Give him a gift that lasts all year, with a series of portraits by photo artist Mark Laurie. Inner Spirit, on the web at inner-spirit-photo.com."

With a fifty-two-week campaign of real stories as told by women, husbands, and boyfriends, Mark began to experience growth almost immediately. His revenue increased 15 percent in the first quarter, and at the end of the first nine months, it had risen 30 percent.

Would this have worked using actors instead of real clients? Not likely, remember, authenticity is key here. With a heightened BS detector, women can spot a fake a mile away. Rehearsed testimonials just don't resonate with the right brain of a woman. Real stories and real people are the key.

Transparency: What Are Your Priorities?

One of the key components to authenticity is *transparency*, or allowing the customer to see every dimension of what you really are: The good, the bad, and the ugly. Transparency has been in the spotlight in recent years thanks to corporate accounting scandals like those at Enron and WorldCom. Financial reporting aside, transparency is also critical to successful marketing and business growth.

In its purest form, transparency can work for *or* against you, depending on how you prioritize your values. Let's look at two companies for whom maintaining low prices is a core value—Wal-Mart and Costco—and the different approach each takes.

Wal-Mart—Always Low Prices

For years, the world's number-one retailer has offered groceries and products under the motto Always Low Prices. Since the death of founder Sam Walton in 1992, however, Wal-Mart has struggled with challenges that have impacted its public image and ability to compete with other retailers.

It's no secret that Wal-Mart is focused on expansion, growth, and category domination. With more than five thousand Wal-Mart and Sam's Club outlets worldwide, it is projected that the company will hold 35 percent of the U.S. grocery store market share by 2007 *(MSNBC.com; August 2005).* But the drive for domination comes at a high cost. The same customers that shop at Wal-Mart have fought publicly to keep the "big box" out of their own neighborhoods. Wal-Mart is often seen as a bully figure, putting mom-and-pop establishments out of business and having no sensitivity about the location of their stores. A recent example can be viewed from atop Mexico's two-thousand-year-old Pyramid of the Sun, less than a mile from the tourist gate in Teotihuacan. Further, the company is mired in litigation stemming from charges of racial and gender discrimination and health-insurance issues. Currently, there are websites solely devoted to increasing the level of transparency of Wal-Mart's practices.

In what has to be the irony of all ironies, Lee Scott, CEO and chairman of Wal-Mart, recently called upon the British government to look into the business practices of Tesco, the U.K. grocery chain that is a direct competitor to Wal-Mart-owned Asda. Declaring an unfair competitive advantage, Scott said, "As you get over 30 percent and higher I am sure there is a point where government is compelled to intervene, particularly in the UK, where you have the planning laws that make it difficult to compete *(The Sunday Times; August 2005).*

With $841 million spent on advertising in 2004 and major market defeats in South Korea and Germany, Wal-Mart is currently struggling to maintain its hold on the retail crown. The company is working to redefine core values and priorities; with retail chains like Target nipping at its heels, Wal-Mart has recently announced a marketing makeover—away from low prices and toward higher-quality product.

Costco—Everyone's a Winner

Jim Sinegal is the CEO of Costco Wholesale, now the fifth-largest retailer in the country. He loves his job, his employees, and his customers. But while creating a retail giant, he's also, as they say in New York, "created such a scandal you never saw," forcing the bigwigs down on Wall Street to "get their undies in a bunch."

Costco puts Wal-Mart to shame in the arena of low pricing. They steadfastly hold to the rule that nothing will be marked up more than 15 percent (compared with competitor's markup of 25 percent and more). They pay their employees an average of seventeen dollars per hour—42 percent higher than Sam's Club—and have one of the best health plans in the industry *(New York Times; July 2005).* The employee turnover rate is nearly nonexistent.

Costco's stock rose more than 10 percent in 2004. What does Wall Street have to say about this? *Jim is too generous.* Analysts have complained that it's better to be an employee or customer than a shareholder. They feel Jim could be charging more for the goods he sells.

Jim has responded: "On Wall Street, they're in the business of making money between now and next Thursday. I don't say that with any bitterness, but we can't take that view. We want to build a company that will still be here fifty and sixty years from now. This is not altruistic. This is good business *(New York Times; July 2005).*

Costco's mission is to sell products to its members at the lowest-possible price. But the company also places its employees and customers above almighty profit. Contrasted with Wal-Mart, this simple difference in priorities shines through in each customer experience. Costco has created cult-like consumer loyalty and $40 billion in revenue with almost no traditional advertising.

Conclusion

Given the choice, today's female consumer is going to do business with a company that doesn't necessarily offer the lowest price or the most convenience; what she's looking for is a relationship based on shared beliefs that resonate through every customer touch point. She wants a clear, honest image of that business in her mind; the more transparent a company is about all aspects of its business, the stronger the brand loyalty.

So, what do you believe? What is it about your business that sets you on fire to embrace every new day? Quick, can you give us a list of three of your core beliefs? And we're wondering about this: If your employees were asked to do the same thing, how closely would their list resemble yours? Are your employees in tune with what you believe? If not, how can you expect your customers to connect with you if your own employees don't?

Women want to know the *real* you. Take some time to think about yourself awhile. Until you really know yourself, you can't really get to know her.

15

The Power of Words:

Connecting with Her Through Effective Copywriting

When it comes to conveying your message and persuading a woman to do business with you, the language you use is key.

- Stop talking about the features of your business and start telling her what it will do for her. Offer solutions to the challenges in her everyday life.
- Use the language of the right brain; touch on the emotional, experiential, nurturing side of the brain so that she "sees" herself in your ad, connects with you, and plants your brand in the "reward behavior" area of her brain.
- Connect with a woman's senses through copy that reflects tastes, smells, and textures. The most organic copywriting is often the most effective.
- Realize that you can't possibly say everything in one piece of copy. Just as you build a strong fortress brick by brick, so must you tell your story. The finer the sliver of information you concentrate on, the more powerful the message.

Finally, always remember there is no such thing as one generic female consumer. Women have different needs at different times, and the language required for each buying mode is quite different.

The Buying Modes of Women

MICHELE: The other day, I was a consumer of many colors.

In the morning, I stopped by Sonora Quest Labs, armed with a form from my doctor. Having blood drawn for medical tests is not my idea of fun, but you do what you gotta do. There are several labs to choose from in the area, but I like Sonora Quest. They have a *huge* office and must process fifty patients an hour—it's a study in operational excellence. Knowing the office runs like a well-oiled (and friendly) machine takes some stress out of having a giant needle stuck in your elbow.

On my way home, I decided to stop by the Apple store. I didn't think I needed anything, but apparently I did, because after hanging out there talking to the Mac geniuses, I left with a pair of JBL speakers. The speakers are cute, but I really dug the bag I carried them home in, which could be carried as a sling or knapsack.

Most of the afternoon was spent in the emergency room of the Mayo Clinic Hospital, thanks to a situation that involved my dog Penny, a hard living room floor, and my husband's rib cage. If you've never been to the Mayo Clinic, you're missing out on how medicine really should be practiced. It's an awesome place to be sick (if you have to be). Waiting for my husband to come out of X-ray, I was amazed to find a young man by the name of Charlie, dressed in a Mayo uniform, walking around the waiting area asking people if they needed anything. He brought bottles of water, newspapers, a remote control for the television set. Charlie was a hero to everyone anxiously waiting for a loved one to finish treatment.

What made this day interesting was that, in each situation, *I was a different consumer*. What drew me to Sonora Quest was the knowledge (and assurance) that patient treatment was based on an efficient, methodical system of operation. I stopped by Apple on the fly with a spontaneous urge to see what cool stuff was available. Even the visit to Mayo left me feeling cared for, with the human touch provided by Charlie.

Throughout the day, I was a Methodical consumer, a Spontaneous consumer and a Humanistic consumer. (We'll talk more about the different types of buying modes shortly.) I had different needs at different times, and these businesses delivered.

How did they know what buying mode I was in? They didn't—they actually cover their bases by doing things that satisfy each type of consumer. I just didn't see them all, for I was only looking for things that satisfied the mode I was in at the moment.

Are you satisfying a small number of consumers over and over, but are stymied as to why you aren't attracting others? It could be you're only marketing to one type of consumer and need to remember individual women have individual needs, and that they will exhibit a varying range of buying modes.

Remember the four women Holly wrote about in chapter 8 who were interested in taking a cruise? If we look at what their individual needs (and buying modes) are, we find that each of them falls into one of four categories. Future Now Inc. developed these buying modes based on techniques like Myers Briggs Type Indicator.

4 Buying Modes

Left Brain (logic)	Right Brain (emotion)
Connie **Competitive** Competence—Control Challenges Success-Oriented	Susan **Spontaneous** Flexibility—Immediacy Exciting Experiences Activity-Oriented
Mary **Methodical** Information—Specifics Organization—Systems Detail-Oriented	Helen **Humanistic** Personal Touch Helping Others Relationship-Oriented

The Four Quadrants represent buying modalities based on whether or not you are more emotional or logical and quick to act or deliberate to act.

There is no such thing as one type of female consumer. In the example showing the review of my average day, my buying-modality shifted from situation to situation. The only way these businesses could have touched me as strongly as they did was by providing experiences that accounted for all four modes. That way, they never had to second-guess what mode I might be in at any given moment.

Take the Mayo Clinic, for example. Reflecting on past visits, I've experienced:

- The extraordinary organization of the administrative system (Methodical).
- Light chamber music presented in the hospital's rotunda by local musicians (Spontaneous).
- State-of-the-art radiation equipment and procedures for cancer treatment (Competitive).
- And, of course, Charlie the Wandering Angel in the emergency room (Humanistic).

Copywriting for Buying Modes

Not only should a customer's experience be developed around buying modes, but copywriting should, too. You must make sure you speak to a female consumer in a language that resonates with her buying mode.

Let's say you run "On-the-Go Gourmet," a kitchen where women come to cook their own family-style gourmet meals. You supply the ingredients, equipment, and clean-up. You want to create a brochure explaining the services you offer. What kind of copy are you going to write that will speak to the needs of individual women?

Mary Methodical

"For the cost of two nights' worth of pizza, On-the-Go Gourmet gives a family of four dinner for a week. With a wide variety of recipes, there's something for everyone. And there's no hassle. We supply everything you need, from ingredients to mixing bowls to mop up. You choose your recipe beforehand, and we'll have everything waiting for you upon your arrival. Just mix, cook, and go!"

Susan Spontaneous
"On-the-Go Gourmet is the exciting new way to try unique, delicious dishes from around the world. Choose your recipe beforehand or pick one to try on a whim when you arrive. On-the-Go Gourmet always has everything you need for every dish in our recipe book. Stop losing sleep over what to feed the family. Spend your time creating instead!"

Helen Humanistic
"Even if you're new to the kitchen, On-the-Go Gourmet makes it easy to be a dinner superhero to your family. We not only have all the ingredients and equipment you need; our cooking experts are on hand to help every step of the way. You'll love working with our 'gourmet sherpas' while you're preparing meals; we're there as much as you need us (be sure to ask about our private tutoring sessions). Success—and a great deal of fun—is guaranteed!"

Connie Competitive
"The award-winning staff of On-the-Go Gourmet has a combined forty years of food experience with some of the finest restaurants in the region. As certified master chefs and teachers, your 'gourmet sherpas' will guide you through an efficient, state-of-the-art cooking process that creates gastronomical masterpieces in record time. It's not just cooking; it's a gourmet meal that will have your family and friends saying, 'How did you *do* that?'"

This is copy that can be used for advertising, brochures, your website and even training material for your staff, to help them understand the different angles of approach each persona takes in encountering the same subject. Once you get in a consistent groove of addressing and providing solutions for individual needs, it will become second nature, for you *and* your staff.

Speaking Her Language Online—Keywords

> *"Studies show we find people more likable and trustworthy when they're like us. Even the word 'rapport' is a clue. Literally, it comes from the French verb rapporter which means 'to bring back.'*
>
> *Rapport is what you have between two people who feel like they can understand each other's feelings or ideas. When the message they send out comes back from that other person as almost identical, or at least in harmony with our own way of thinking."*
>
> — John Forde from *The Copywriter's Roundtable* (www.jackforde.com)

Are you speaking your customer's language? Are you listening to the messages she is sending out? Are you repeating that message back to her? It's an excellent way to build rapport. Rapport is the first step in building your relationship with the women you want to become your customers.

So what language is she speaking? How does she describe her needs, and the problems or solutions she is seeking? This is incredibly important for two reasons:

1. When your copy speaks to a customer in her language, it is more persuasive.
2. The words she uses to describe her needs, problems, or solutions are the words she's typing into search engines. They are the keywords for which she'll find you. Target the keywords she's using, and you'll get more qualified traffic to your website.

Many companies suffer from an "inside the bottle" approach. The language and terminology the company uses may not be the same as the vocabulary she uses. Wherever possible, get rid of the techno-speak and simplify your terminology and copy.

This is not to say "dumb down" your copy. She will sense if you are being condescending.

Avoid Techno-Speak

> *"We want to be known as the human capital management solutions resource."*
>
> *"When you think integrated component technology applications—think Brand XYZ."*
>
> *"We're going to name the new suite of services Technology Synergy products."*

Here's the problem.

These aren't the words your customers are using to describe what they need, what their problems are, or what they're looking for. They're not looking for "human capital management solutions;" they're looking for a staffing company. They're not typing "human capital management solutions" into search engines. They're typing "staffing company" or "staffing services."

From a search engine standpoint, of course you want to include the words or phrases customers use to describe their needs, and the problems, or solutions they are seeking. But these visitors will also respond when you use their vocabulary on your website.

Holly did an online copywriting job for a client who was previously using a lot of techno-speak phrases. She rewrote the copy using more simple language, using the language of their customers. The result? Conversion went from a trickle of leads a month to a flood. It's the first time she's ever had a client respond to the results of a project by saying they were "doing cartwheels." Now, keep in mind, there were also changes made in design and linking that also helped tremendously. But the copy did make a big difference.

Are you speaking your customer's language? It affects everything you do from the copy on your website to the design of your product.

Take Intuit, the big tax and business software company. Their software product, Simple Start, a basic accounting package, went through many iterations. The initial "aging reports" and "invoicing" were edited out. Accounts receivable became "Money In," accounts payable, "Money Out." The SnapTax divisions hired an editor from People magazine to help translate accountant-speak into real-world language.

You may be thinking, *"But what about the men on my site. They want those high tech words and phrases. If I don't include them, I'll lose credibility with my male and more knowledgeable customers."*

There is a way to do both. Let's take a fairly technical product, rugged military computers. Here's an example of a company using techno-jargon:

> *XYZ Computers is uniquely qualified and properly positioned to deliver real COTS systems in real time. For years, we've been a primary choice of systems integrators and OEMs searching for economical, high-performance solutions to the challenges our industry presents. Drawing on a rich pool of talent and experience, a solid relationship with our suppliers, and a commitment to the successful execution of the concept of COTS in mission-critical applications, our reputation—and our customer base—has grown.*

Now here's an example of a company who speaks in a more clear, relatable manner:

> *When you need military computers that are built tough inside and out, AMREL is the clear choice. For those needing fully rugged notebooks, tablets, and PDAs to use in mission critical situations, AMREL has the perfect arsenal. Whether monitoring supplies at a remote base, completing tactical maneuvers, or a technician upgrading the infrastructure, AMREL has the solutions to keep you connected, no matter where the mission takes you.*

Notice that they are still using technical terms—*upgrading the infrastructure, fully rugged notebooks, tablets and PDAs, mission critical situations,* but they are speaking in a more customer-based language. Notice the difference in the "we" based language in the first example, and the "you" based language in the second.

Here's the added benefit: When you speak more clearly with less techno-jargon, you relate better to *all* your customers, men and women.

How to Choose Your Keywords

Your customers sometimes have unique ways of describing things. When Holly's girly-girlfriend was feeling macho and wanted to hang a window flower box outside, she promptly marched up to her boyfriend and asked to borrow his "whirry whirry screw thing . . .you know . . .vroom"—not the technically correct name, but he knew exactly what she was talking about.

How else might she describe what she needs? An electric drill, an electric screwdriver, a power drill, a power tool, a battery-operated screwdriver?

When you're trying to find your best keywords, keep two things in mind. One, what is the visitor's intention? Two, how does the visitor describe your product? It may be different from the terms you use internally.

Find Your Best Keywords Tip #1—Visitor Intention

What is the intention of the person typing in the keyword? Women-owned businesses are growing at an exponential rate. Many of these women business owners are opening up offices or stores and need phones. A woman business owner typing in "phone systems," a broad term, may be early in the buying process. What does she often see? A landing page with tons of techno-speak or a page displaying lots of products with no text to help her choose which one might be right for her, as we saw in our earlier example.

Wouldn't it be nice to be taken to a page that explains what the different phone systems are and which options might be best for a small business owner?

Now—a woman business owner typing in "IP-PBX phone system" has probably done a lot more homework. She knows a specific type of phone system. She's further along in the buying process. Now is a good time to take her to a specific phone system. To find your best keywords, understand what your visitor's intention is.

Find Your Best Keywords Tip #2—Words Your Visitors Use to Describe What They Need

How a customer describes your product may be very different from terms you use internally.

We have a client, The Sedona Method (Sedona.com), who sells a self-help releasing technique. A huge issue for women is what they term "emotional trauma." Upon further exploration, we found emotional trauma could be broken down into lots of other terms: Grief, caretaker's syndrome, co-dependency, martyr syndrome, low self-esteem. The other problem with trying to find your best keywords that some visitors do not recognize their true condition. A martyr thinks she is a self-sacrificing saint, and that's a good thing. "Martyr" strikes her as a negative label she would never give herself. So we had to delve deeper: What do women with this syndrome suffer from? The answer was sleep deprivation and lack of energy—so we targeted those keywords.

Go out there and find your best keywords. Keep in mind, different personas may have different needs, motivations, and buying processes. The time you spend researching will be well-rewarded by attracting qualified traffic to your site.

Conclusion

Start thinking about the power of language in the messages you convey and the words you use. Tap into the right brain by displaying imagination, and showing authenticity, and help her to see herself in your marketing and advertising.

Everything you do and say is a language, and the ways you speak to the different buying modes of customers are all separate but equal dialects. Neglect a dialect and you alienate a large segment of the population. Ongoing awareness of and attention to *all* dialects means you'll have whatever she needs, whenever she needs it, and you'll also have a clear-cut strategy for exponential growth.

Authenticity, transparency, and the power of words. Stripped to its essence, the message is, as renowned copywriter John Forde would put it, "fewer ideas, more passionately-held." Convey that passion to your customers in everything you do, from the relevance of your marketing messages to the cleanliness of your restrooms.

16

The World Inside Your Door:

How Personas Help Create Powerful Customer Experiences

MICHELE: "I've done everything possible to create good relationships with my female patients," a physician announced during one of my recent seminars. "I've decorated my office with marble pillars and resort-style furniture. I've painted the rooms soothing colors and have a Japanese fountain in the waiting room to calm the nerves. There are a variety of magazines on the coffee table that appeal to different personalities. I even have a corner coffee café where women can make themselves a cappuccino." He leaned back in his chair. "When it comes to marketing to women, I've covered all the bases. You can't possibly add anything—there's *nothing* left."

I let his statement hang like Air Jordan for a few ticks of the clock, then arched an eyebrow and asked, "How long do your patients have to sit in the waiting room before they're escorted in to see you?"

It was like hitting him with a two-by-four. Waiting time is one of the most important aspects of the patient experience, yet he hadn't seen it. Rather than interior decorating or refreshments, think how much more effective it would have been to focus on eliminating the biggest complaint patients have these days—interminable waits in small rooms with no windows and no explanation.

This doctor had a good start in reaching out to female patients. So what prevented him from achieving the ultimate customer experience? *He was thinking about what he should offer rather than the actual needs of individuals.*

When it comes to marketing, businesses often focus on one or two areas like advertising or customer service, believing that if these things are done well enough, customers will connect with them for life. In fact, advertising and customer service are only two spokes in the giant Wheel of Persuasion:

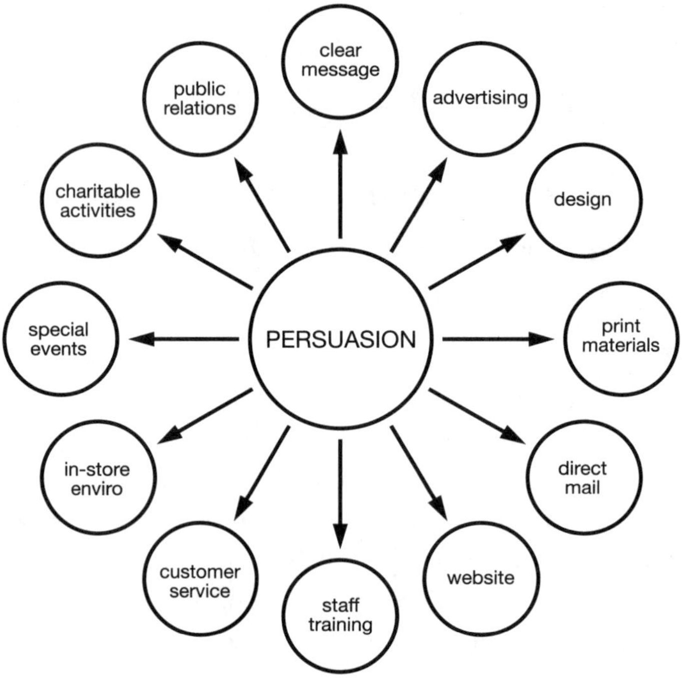

If you view persuasion as the hub of your marketing strategy, you see how critical each of the spokes is to the whole. Ignore, weaken, or break a spoke and the entire strategy will not only under perform, it could even collapse.

Every touch point the customer has with you sends a message about your business. It can be your advertising, the location of your store or the way your staff answers the phone. It can be the usability of your website, the cleanliness of your bathrooms, or the lighting in your parking lot. And yes, it definitely is how long your customer is forced to wait before being served. She is affected by each and every interaction with you, whether it is physical, emotional, or virtual. It's up to you to make sure her experiences are positive on a consistent basis and serve the individual needs of your personas.

You Talkin' to Me?

Not only do you have to make sure you're delivering your utmost in each area of your business, you have to do so in a way that speaks to each persona. Let's look at the doctor example again. You probably agreed when we said endless waits in physicians' offices were one of the biggest complaints patients have. But did you realize that *each persona has a different reason for the same complaint?* Think back to the cruise example in the chapter on personas and what makes each buying mode tick. Mary Methodical is irritated by the lack of organization and attention to detail. Susan Spontaneous wishes someone would come out into the waiting room to tell her why the wait is so long and how much longer it will be. Helen Humanistic is upset about being ignored, but being a people-pleaser, she feels she cannot complain. This only irritates her further. And Connie Competitive is seething because she's dealing with incompetence and now feels like she's lost control of her entire day.

It would be a good start for the doctor to say, "I'm going to make sure my patients don't have to wait long in the waiting room, or if we're running behind, make sure we tell them why." But is it good *enough*? Until the doctor and his staff *really* understand how and why each individual persona is affected, their solution won't become ingrained in the overall marketing strategy.

Integrating Personas into Your Marketing Strategy

Spend some time with the Wheel of Persuasion and review how your business performs on each spoke of the wheel. When it comes to messaging, or copywriting, you've already seen some examples in the last chapter with the Gourmet-On-the-Gourmet copy. You didn't just write basic copy to address a mass market; you took the time to address the specific needs and deeper motivations of Mary, Susan, Helen, and Connie.

It's up to you to give as much attention to each spoke in the Wheel of Persuasion as you've given to creating a message that resonates with individual needs. The total customer experience is your target, an experience that means different things to different women.

Aligning Every Spoke in the Wheel

Each spoke in the Wheel of Persuasion relies on the strength of its personas. Approach everything in your business with personas in mind and you'll have a rock-solid marketing strategy.

Let's take another spoke on the wheel. Try applying the persona process to your in-store (or office) environment, as Michele did recently with one of her clients.

> MICHELE: House of Critters, a pet store in Anchorage, Alaska, takes pet ownership very seriously. With a background in the veterinary sciences, the owners and staff are highly protective of the animals they have for sale and go to great lengths to prevent exposure to unnecessary germs and disease. The problem was, the store was *so* clean and neat, so pristine, that it gave off a very antiseptic atmosphere. It felt as if you were walking into a hospital.
>
> Customers complained because of the strict rules enforced by the store's employees, including no tapping on the glass and no holding an animal unless you were serious about purchasing it. Even then, you were required to sanitize your hands with antibacterial gel before entering and exiting the animal room.
>
> We realized that people were reacting negatively to the strict rules and regulations because *no one had ever explained the reasoning behind the policy to customers.* We set out to make some small but significant changes to the in-store environment.
>
> We hired an illustrator to create large animal cartoon cutouts and placed them on the walls of designated pet areas. Each cartoon animal was given something important to say, explaining

to customers why certain rules existed. The puppy cartoon, for example, said, "Please don't tap on the glass, we're just babies and sometimes it frightens us. We know you think we're cute. We think you're pretty cute, too!" We then duplicated the cartoons (without the quotes) and hung them over the appropriate section of the store to match the animal with the supplies they'd need.

To rid the store of the antiseptic smell, we installed a rotating system of air fresheners. Sometimes the smell would be cedar, other times a citrus aroma. We changed the lighting in the store from fluorescent tubes to fixtures that more readily resemble natural daylight (a big plus in dark, wintry Anchorage). For pet owners who wanted more of the personal touch, we built a customer care center, complete with pet-care brochures, a television with video library, and regularly scheduled how-to sessions on everything from clipping your cat's nails to setting up a freshwater fish tank. We also created a "new and cool" product wall adjacent to the checkout counter, highlighting new pet-care and gift items. The response from customers was immediate and overwhelming. After twenty years in business, the store finally made the connection with the needs of its customers.

House of Critters integrated the needs of personas into every element of the business: Organization and detail for Methodicals; interesting "adventures" like seminars and "new and cool" product walls for Spontaneous types; a customer care center to help a Humanistic types; and highly efficient, cutting-edge customer service for Competitives. Hard work? Indeed. But the result was exponential growth in a very short period of time—23 percent in the first year.

Give Your Staff a Turn at the Wheel

Doing a comprehensive job of consistently delivering on each element of your marketing strategy is a major challenge; customizing that delivery to match the needs of different personas can at first seem impossible. It is overwhelming and you can't do it alone. You must, and should, look for opportunities where your staff can step in and take charge.

When we mention this to clients, their first reaction is to say, "I don't have anyone who can handle all these responsibilities." Of course they don't. No one person exists who can do everything. The key is to share the wealth. Each person on your staff should have some kind of marketing responsibility that matches the strengths of his or her own personality.

Getting to know your staff is just like getting to know female consumers, you need to work from the inside out. In the workplace, your team members or employees wear "masks" that are quite different from who they really are in their personal lives. They are used to putting on a game face, and while they work hard, their individual preferences and strengths may not be obvious.

There are a couple of things you can do to uncover the strengths of the people you work with, including private conversations to discover if an individual is happy in her job and what she'd really like to be doing. But for a solid, honest answer to the question of individual strengths, you may want to consider having potential and current employees complete a questionnaire that tests for personality-type preferences.

Many successful companies today rely on tests like the Myers-Briggs Type Indicator (MBTI) to determine the personality-type preferences of employees and job candidates. By understanding the strengths of each personality type, it's easier to see whether a job candidate matches specific job requirements or if an employee needs to be transferred to a position that better suits his preferences.

By using this tool to match the right people with the right jobs, companies have saved millions of dollars in hiring and human resources costs. The result is lower turnover, greater productivity, and increased profit.

Personality-type tests give you a sketch of who your employees really are and what their individual "personal preferences" might be. Their answers will reveal:

- Whether they get their energy internally (introvert) or from the external world around them (extrovert).
- How they gather information—abstractly (intuitive) or with concrete data (sensing).
- How they make decisions—with their heads (thinking) or their hearts (feeling).

- How they structure their lives—by organized planning (judging) or spontaneous flexibility (perceiving).

Now, apply the personal preferences of your team to the Wheel of Persuasion. How do their strengths fit in, and in what areas of marketing might they excel?

In the case of our physician from the beginning of this chapter, he knew there were two administrative assistants who were not realizing their potential to the fullest—the receptionist and the filing specialist. The receptionist, who had been there for about a year, was doing an acceptable job of making appointments and organizing paperwork, but her bedside manner left a little to be desired. She just didn't seem to connect with female patients on a personal level. The other assistant, an insurance filing specialist, was pleasant enough, but always seemed behind in filing insurance claims and keeping the computer system up-to-date. By giving these two assistants a personality-type preference quiz, it quickly became evident that the receptionist was an ISTJ (introverted, sensing, thinking, judging) and the insurance specialist was an ENFP (extroverted, intuitive, feeling, perceiving). It was easy to see that an experiment in moving the receptionist into the specialist position (where she could work by herself and supervise a timely system of insurance claims) and the specialist into reception (where she could use her people skills) would prove fruitful.

Was this marketing? You bet it was. The new receptionist had just what women needed, a friendly voice over the phone and an intuitive, feeling attitude when caring for them in the waiting room. And the new file clerk could utilize her organizational skills to create a highly efficient insurance claim system that put these busy female patients' minds at ease. The doctor had happy employees with jobs that suited their personality preferences, and, as a result, happy patients.

Real-Life Example: The Boulders

HOLLY: So I'm standing in the hall, anxious to get started. I look over and see a short, stocky man walking toward me. He introduces himself with a firm handshake and an Eastern European accent. I look him up and down and hesitantly reply, "Um . . .Hi."

Why this reticent reaction to a perfectly lovely man? Because he was going to be *standing on my back* for the next seventy minutes. I had taken the plunge and signed up for the Ashiatsu massage. I was expecting a svelte Asian woman. But instead, I got Jovan. True to form, my initial fears were unfounded. Jovan had a wonderful touch (who knew toes could feel so much like fingers), and my shoulders haven't felt this good in years.

There was something about the Golden Door Spa at The Boulders Resort in Arizona that inspired confidence to try new things. I was there on business, working on this book with Michele. I was surprised at how much I thoroughly enjoyed The Boulders. After my smorgasbord of spa treatments, I came home rested and relaxed. The same could not be said, however, for my credit card. It was exhausted from over-exertion and in desperate need of some rest itself. Last I saw it, it gave me a nasty look, said it had a headache, and was heading to bed. Ah . . . but it was worth every penny.

So I was trying to figure out why I had such a positive experience at this place. I've stayed in nice resorts before, so why did this one stand out?

Many of you may have heard of the Broken Windows theory. It was applied to fighting crime. The theory was things left unfixed give the impression no one is in charge and no one cares. But the same theory has been applied to business, both in little things left unfixed, and in the little ways you go above and beyond what is expected.

I believe this is vitally important, especially with your female customers. Because of the wiring of their brains (more connections between the two hemispheres) and their traditional roles as caretakers and multitaskers, women notice everything, even small things, good or bad. If you want her business, everything matters, so you must pay attention to the details.

I think that's why The Boulders impressed me so much. All things compared, the setting, rooms, and amenities were on par with many other resorts I've visited. What made it memorable and remarkable were all the little touches.

- Each night, the staff provided a "turn down" service, where they left a sample of a different Golden Door Spa product. One night, it was a lavender oil, another a rejuvenation cream, another a lip balm. I looked forward to going back to my room to see what goodie they'd left me. (This is also a wonderful opportunity to promote product sales by giving away free samples.)

- The Boulders charges you one fee daily which covers all tipping (except for meals and spa services). At first, I wasn't too crazy about this. But after catching rides on the shuttle, or asking bell people to bring me ice or extra firewood, it was actually nice not to have to worry about the correct amount to tip or having cash at the ready.
- When you play golf, rental clubs come with two free sleeves of balls, and the starter prepares a to-go cup of fresh lemon ice water and puts it in your cart for you.
- The cactus plants that decorate the interior lodge all have name tags that tell you what kind of cactus plant each one is. The same is true for many of the plants along the walkways. This may sound strange to some people, but for a constantly learning geek like me, it was great to know what the different cacti were and what plants I was admiring.
- The employees never made you wait. There were swarms of people running around with earpieces, a la secret service. They constantly called one another, so there was never a long wait to get a shuttle bus or a golf cart to one of the property restaurants or to get someone to help with your bags.
- Everyone was nice: The people who answered the phones, the guy who fixed a blown fuse, the yoga instructors, and the guy who came to build a fire every day. Even the wild boar who were enjoying their dinner of fresh fairway grass were unperturbed by my only decent drive of the day which nearly took one out, and they did not slap one another on the back and laugh when I hit my next ball into the water. Even the resort animals were courteous.

All those seemingly small, often simple things added up to a superior experience. Women notice everything. If you're doing something wrong, fix it immediately. It's making a bigger impact than you think. And if you really want to be remarkable, try doing a little something extra. Those little things can add up to a big difference in your bottom line.

Real Life Website Example: Beautyhabit.com

HOLLY: The same principle that goes into personal customer experience applies to your website. What is the total customer experience offered by your company or website? We've talked about the importance of every touch point. On the Internet, it's the importance of every single click. How far do you go not only to satisfy your customers, but truly *delight* them? What's the difference between satisfying and delighting? Often it can be simply one or two extra efforts, something the customer isn't necessarily expecting. Beautyhabit.com did just that for me.

First of all, they satisfied me. Here's the scenario. A friend had given me a gift of Eskandar Jojoba and Olive Oil Moisturizing Body Milk. I loved the stuff. When my bottle ran out, I wanted more. I carefully saved the bottle so I'd know the exact name of the product. Of course, I then threw it without writing down the information.

So I went to Google and typed in "Eskandar" since that's all I could really remember.

This brought up the following results:

Neiman Marcus - Apparel for Her - Fine Apparel - **eskandar**
Visit NeimanMarcus.com for **eskandar** featuring new collections from top designers, such as **eskandar**. NeimanMarcus.com has fashion's top names in clothing, ...
www.neimanmarcus.com/.../EntryP.jhtml?itemId=cat000025&parentId=cat000019&masterId=cat000009 - 57k - Cached - Similar pages

eskandar
Beautyhabit stocks the complete **eskandar** bath and body range.
www.beautyhabit.com/**eskandar**.html - 23k - Cached - Similar pages

The Stylephile: Escape to **Eskandar** (NYC)
Eskandar's home collection Devout fans of London-based designer **Eskandar** will no longer have to suffer the company of Bergdorf Blondes to stock up on his ...
weblogs.variety.com/the_style_phile/ 2005/02/escape_to_eskan.html - 23k - Cached - Similar pages

Eskandar Women's Clothing - Clothing & Accessories - BizRate ...
Buy **Eskandar** Women's Clothing from Clothing & Accessories stores. Compare prices & shop online at BizRate. Check store ratings before you buy Women's ...
www.bizrate.com/womensclothing/ brand--**eskandar**/products__att259--279994-.html - 67k - Cached - Similar pages

'vE-"jA:: The most anticipated VJ Book of the decade!!
'vE-"jA: Art + Technology of Live Audio-Video is a global snapshot of an exploding genre of

Eskandar
Up to 50% off **Eskandar!**
Compare prices and save money.
www.everysell.com

Eskandar
Save on **Eskandar**
Compare **Eskandar** & prices
www.Shopping.com

Now, Neiman Marcus had an advantage, since it was a brand name I recognized. But when I looked at the text, it was discussing clothing items. I wanted a moisturizer, so I clicked on the link to beautyhabit.com.

Here's the landing page that came up:

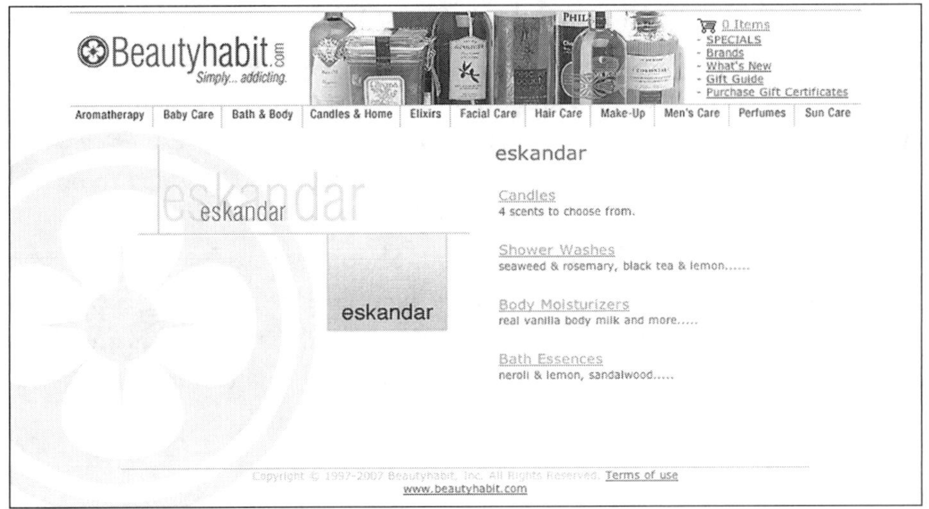

My keyword, Eskandar, was in big bold letters all over the top of the page. Perfect. I was definitely in the right place. And I had an easy choice, "Body Moisturizers," to continue my scent trail. That click took me to this page:

Here's where I had to stop and think. The "Order" and "Checkout" buttons both had equal weighting as far as size. The only difference was color. What I really wanted to do was check out, but did I have to order first? I know this may have some of you going "Duh," but I'm telling you, *never make your customers think*. Always make it completely obvious what to do next. I wanted to order it AND I wanted to check out, so which would be better to click?

I clicked "Order," which took me to the "Shopping Cart."

Beautyhabit.com does a lot of things right in this shopping cart. I love the information at the top that lets you know exactly when orders are placed and shipped. I love that they have a phone number you can call. I love that they show you tax and shipping right away so you can get a real idea of the total cost.

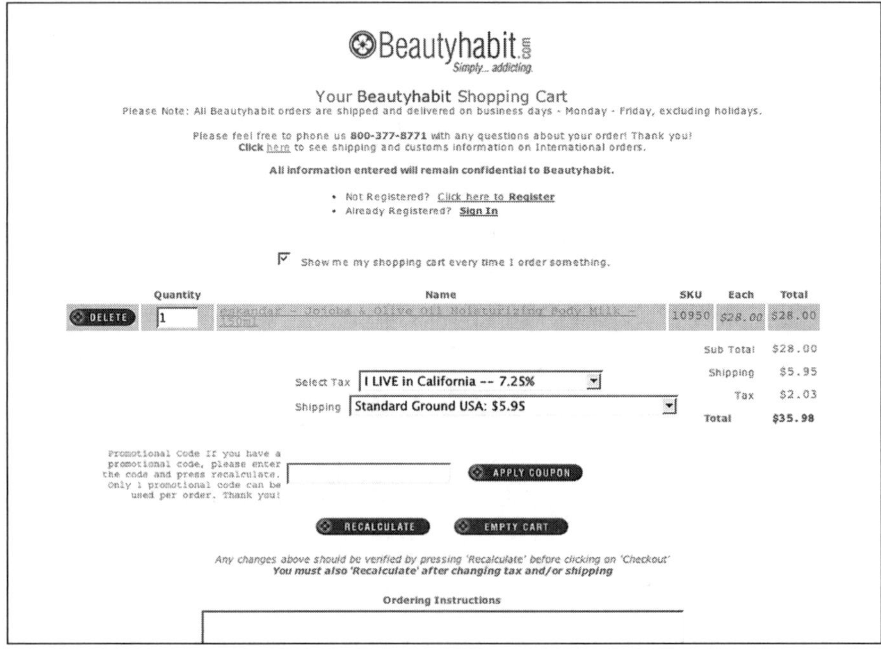

But there's a problem here. The main calls to action in my active window were "Apply Coupon," "Recalculate," and "Empty Cart." Huh? I wanted to check out. How do I do that? I wondered. Well, here's what happened. The main call to action was way down at the bottom of the page, and, in the case of my browser window, *not visible*.

Total $35.98

Promotional Code If you have a promotional code, please enter the code and press recalculate. Only 1 promotional code can be used per order. Thank you!

APPLY COUPON

RECALCULATE EMPTY CART

Any changes above should be verified by pressing 'Recalculate' before clicking on 'Checkout'
You must also 'Recalculate' after changing tax and/or shipping

Ordering Instructions

If you have a gift certificate, enter the number and PIN then press Redeem Certificate
Number: PIN: REDEEM CERTIFICATE

Select payment type: Visa

CONTINUE SHOPPING CHECKOUT

Don't forget! If you live **OUTSIDE** of California, change the tax field.

Here's another problem: Now that I'd scrolled down the page, I had no less than six calls to action (buttons), all equally weighted. It would be helpful if the "Checkout" button was much larger, in a different color, or otherwise designed to stand out as the main call to action.

The checkout process went pretty smoothly. There are a few other things I really like: I like the fact that they don't automatically place a check mark in the "Sign me up for Beautyhabit Special Offers and a Catalog!" Now, from a business point of view, many websites automatically opt you into their e-mail list. The box is pre-checked so that they will get more subscribers. *However, from a brand point of view, allowing customers to opt in rather than opt out is a relationship builder*. Something else to think about here is that many legitimate customers cry "Spam!" when you send them stuff, even though they did not uncheck the box. They are legally opted in to your list. But it feels like spam and they may even report you for spamming them.

Payment -- Credit Card

Select payment type: Visa
Card Number
Card Verification Value (required) (How to Find My Credit Card Verification Number)
Name on Card
Company
Expiration Date Jan. 2006

Sign me up for Beautyhabit Special Offers and a Catalog!

RETURN TO CART SUBMIT THIS ORDER

I got the usual confirmation e-mail. But here's where Beautyhabit.com went above and beyond. Some companies will inform you when your order has been shipped. Terrific. But I have not found many, in my experience, that tell you when it has arrived. Here is the e-mail I received telling me that my package was at my side door.

They told me what time it was delivered, and even where! I *loved* this! I had been busy upstairs and had not heard the delivery arrive. Another plus is, if you are on the road a lot, as I am, and you get this e-mail, you could immediately call your neighbor and say, "Hey, I just got a package delivered. Could you go by and put it in the garage?" How cool.

At the request of BEAUTY HABIT this notice is to confirm that the following shipment has been delivered.

Important Delivery Information

Delivery Date / Time: 27 June-2006 12:48 PM
Driver Release Location: SIDE DOOR

Shipment Detail

Ship To:
HOLLY BUCHANAN

UPS Service: GROUND
Weight: 1.0 LBS

Tracking Number: IZV94W960348287014
Reference Number 1: 98341
Reference Number 2: **Thank You For Your Order!!

Beautyhabit.com also delighted me by the package itself. Sometimes these things are sent with piss-poor wrapping, packaging materials, etc. Not this one. My plastic bottle, even though it was obviously not fragile, was carefully enclosed in bubble wrap and nestled in a sea of foam peanuts. It was obvious beautyhabit.com had taken great care in the packaging and shipping.

And here's my favorite: They included a little plastic bag tied up in a ribbon with sample products and a *hand-written* note, "Holly, Thank you and enjoy!—Lauren."

Now, these were simple little touches, but they made the difference between my being satisfied and being delighted. By the way, when I called the 800 number just to see what the experience would be like, a real live person answered—no waiting, no impossible menus to navigate. She was polite and helpful. What a treat. Rather than outsourcing to a call center, Beautyhabit.com has trained employees answering the phone.

So, other than a few minor hiccups, the whole experience, from Google search result to arrival of the product, was a positive one. I am now a loyal beautyhabit.com customer.

Conclusion

What are you doing not only to satisfy but delight your customers? Are you looking at every touch point, every interaction, every click on your website? Are you creating personas and making sure each one has a positive total customer experience?

Remember, everything is marketing. But you don't have to do it alone. The art of balancing a complete marketing strategy takes time and practice. Trust us, as long as you give yourself enough time, keep your eye on the big picture, and assemble a strong team to pay attention to every detail, you'll not only have more customers, you'll have happier, more *loyal customers.*

PART VI

The Future of Marketing to Women

17

Customer Empowerment:

The Importance of Staying Ahead of the Curve

On January 27, 2006, director Steven Soderbergh's film *Bubble* made history when it was released in movie theaters *and* on television the very same night. The groundbreaking event was the brainchild of Mark Cuban, owner of the Dallas Mavericks basketball team and HDNet, the high-definition cable channel.

It's easy to guess the reaction of Hollywood executives, who have lived and died by the traditional film-distribution business model since time began. Imagine then, the virtual tailspin they found themselves in when, four days later, *Bubble* was *also* released on DVD.

"This just isn't the way things are done," studio executives cried, jumping up and down. "You're breaking tradition, destroying the movie theatre business." But Cuban and Soderbergh held their ground, maintaining that only a small percentage of today's public actually chooses to see films in movie theaters. For a variety of reasons, the majority of people wait for release on cable or DVD. So, they asked, why not give everyone what they want, when they want it? *(Note: as compensation, 1 percent of DVD sales went to theatre owners agreeing to show the film, so everybody won.)* The experiment was enough of a success that

Cuban and Soderbergh have announced similar plans for several more films in coming months.

Now, shrink your television screen down to the size of a cell phone. In your hand, you hold the platform for a product called ScanBuy, a small but powerful consumer tool that's generating tremors throughout the retail world. Go to ScanBuy's website, download the free software into your cell phone, and the next time you're in a retail store, use the camera in your phone to take a photo of a product's bar code. ScanBuy's system will check it over the Internet and respond back to your phone with lightning speed, telling you *where you can get it cheaper*. And, if it's less expensive online, there's likely to be a link for ordering it right there on the spot. One click of your cell phone's enter button and the product is on its way to your doorstep.

Holy Cow—what's happening here?

These are just two examples of the dozens of new products, software, and services announced *every day* in the news. The world of developing technology is in hyper-drive and shows no signs of slowing. Changes in the way we do business may seem subtle at the moment, but the scale of power is undeniably (and permanently) tipping in the direction of the consumer. With advances in technology and social media—like blogs, e-mail and customer reviews—customer empowerment is on the rise. And with eighty cents of every dollar either influenced or directly spent by a woman, this means female customer empowerment.

In the twenty-first century, customization and individual preference are the stars that guide the good ship *Future,* and women are finding it rather easy to adapt their habits to this change in course. Customization. Individualization. Hmmm. Sound familiar? The development of new technologies and communication is the final piece of the puzzle as to why it's important to start marketing to women as consumers with individual needs and motivations. Fortunately, the set of personas and scenarios you've created in mapping out your marketing strategy will help make your transition into the marketing of tomorrow that much easier.

Your new competition is information, product, and service on-demand. You may not have thought much about what it's going to mean for your business, but guess what? It's here. Standing right behind you, in fact, about to tap you on the shoulder and ask you kindly to play or move out of the way.

Like it or not, delivery by means of technology is going to play a big role in marketing budgets of the future. At the very least, you should be aware of what's going on, and how it's changing the way consumers interact with products and services.

We haven't seen the death of traditional advertising and marketing—yet. But newspaper readership is on the decline. There's an entire generation out there that's never cracked open the Yellow Pages. Internet search engines like Yahoo! or Google are the new tools of consumers. Sirius and XM, the satellite radio services, now come fully installed on many new automobiles. Digital video recorders like TiVo practically eliminate television ads in one fell swoop.

With the iPod revolution and iTunes, you no longer have to buy a CD to get the one song that actually rocks—pick and choose at will. But that's just a start. Breaking down media into small bits for consumption, called "microchunking" by *Business 2.0* magazine, is the wave of the future for video, as well. Download your favorite episode of *Law & Order* for $1.99 or check out Comedy Central's MotherLoad, a website that offers segments of the *Daily Show* the morning after an episode airs.

Welcome to the Internet as it was meant to be—the ultimate, customizable tool for each and every individual on the planet. Social media like blogs, wikis, MySpace, FaceBook, Flickr, and YouTube are simply the foundation. This is the new era of extreme customer empowerment, and it will affect how you do business, starting *today*. No matter what the size of your business, you must start integrating technology and social media into your marketing. What opportunities are out there for you? The more you know today, the more competitive you'll be tomorrow.

Say you own a garden and landscaping center in a medium-size town in the Midwest. Did you know Home Depot has a community-based garden center section on its website, complete with planting instructions, project guides, and landscaping assistance? That's heavy competition. Why not take control of what you're already doing and make it accessible to your customers? Videotape your landscaping seminars and offer them online. Better yet, microchunk the seminar into five-minute, downloadable video segments, so the customer can watch at her leisure. Put downloadable PDF versions of planting and project guides on your site that she can print out and have on hand when she needs them.

Are you an event-based business? Don't just put a calendar of events up on your website. Follow the example of the Kennedy Center for the Performing Arts. Website visitors can view the events calendar by week or month, and when they find an event that interests them, the event can be automatically transferred to the visitor's Microsoft Outlook calendar with one click of the mouse.

Beware the addictions to the traditional way of advertising. The inability to break away from what you know, combined with rising costs and diminishing returns, can be fatal to your business.

Diminishing Returns on Traditional Advertising

HOLLY: Oh no. I'm standing in a clothing boutique when I happen to glance over and see they have a penny candy section. I immediately start to sweat. What if . . .they have *them.* What if I glance over and see the telltale red shape. Uh oh . . .I'm in trouble. They do have them . . .lots of them. I feel myself starting to lose control.

They say when you get in a situation like this to remove yourself from it, walk away, call a friend for support, call your sponsor. Unfortunately, I don't have a sponsor. You see, I am addicted to . . .Swedish Fish. As of yet, I have not found a Swedish Fish Anonymous support group, so I've been battling this addiction on my own . . .without much success.

Usually I buy them in the big bags, but in the case of this store, they were individually wrapped. I guess the idea is people only buy one or two at a time.

I picked up thirty-seven. (Feeling somewhat guilty, I did leave a handful in the box.)

How do you know you're addicted to something? You have uncontrollable cravings. You increase the amount of intake with diminishing returns.

The feeling from Madison Avenue is, advertisers are addicted to traditional advertising mediums. One such medium is television. Advertisers keep buying it up despite increasing prices and diminishing returns.

McKinsey & Co. has a new report that predicts that by 2010, traditional television advertising will be one-third as effective as it was in 1990. McKinsey is estimating "a 15 percent decrease in buying power, driven by cost-per-thousand rate increases; a 23 percent decline in ads viewed due to switching off; a 9 percent loss of attention to ads due to increased multitasking and a 37 percent decrease in message impact due to saturation."

Television isn't alone in the diminishing returns department. People are tuning out intrusive "push" media. The good news is, they are tuning in participatory "pull" media such as . . .your website.

The Consumer Is in Control

> *"In traditional interruption marketing, the marketer talks directly to as many consumers as possible, with no intermediary other than the media company. The goal of the consumer is to avoid hearing from the advertiser. The goal of the marketer is to spend money buying ads that interrupt people who don't want to be talked to."*
>
> — Seth Godin
> *Unleashing the Idea Virus*

If there is one thing you need to know about how advertising has changed, it is this: The consumer is in control. More and more, mainstream advertising is becoming less and less effective.

So is there any good news? Yes, there are several important forms of marketing that are increasing in popularity and effectiveness. We'll be looking specifically at the Internet, blogs and word-of-mouth marketing.

The Internet, for the most part, is not interruption marketing. Pop-ups and banner ads are interrupters, and their decline in effectiveness proves it. But when a consumer is on the Internet, she is in control. She chooses which websites she wants to go to. She chooses where on the website she wants to go. She decides how long to stay. It's not like a television ad where she's forced to sit through it in order to get to what she wants (the television show). The consumer controls every second of the experience. If she doesn't want to listen to what you have to say, one click of the mouse and she's gone.

Conclusion

We'll talk more about the Internet and how men and women use the Internet differently. There are unique opportunities to market to women on the Internet. But first, let's look at one of the most effective forms of advertising, word of mouth, and how the Internet has made it even stronger than ever.

18

Word-of-Mouth Advertising:

More Powerful Than Ever

The other form of marketing that everyone is talking about (no pun intended) is word-of-mouth marketing. It sounds like an oxymoron. Word of mouth is something you can't control, right? You can't make one person go out and tell another about your product. Consumers are in control. Marketing is something the company or advertiser controls. So how does this work?

Marketers can control the *trigger:* The action, event, website, or ad campaign that starts consumers talking. They can set up touch points to try to reach "influencers" and get them to spread the message. They can provide the vehicles to make it easier to spread the word. But it is consumers who will control the *message* they spread and *who* they spread it to.

Word-of-mouth marketing is a perfect fit for marketing to women. Women have been expert word-of-mouth marketers since the beginning of time. While "hunter and gatherer" men often prefer to make solo decisions, "family caretaker" women have always relied on their network and community to share experiences and help make important decisions.

You need look no further than Mary Kay, Avon, and Tupperware parties to see how marketers have been tapping into word of mouth with huge success.

Ask any woman how she found her hairdresser, plumber, OB-GYN, new outfit, favorite new band or television show and she'll probably reply, "My friend told me about . . ."

Word of mouth (WOM) may be the single most powerful form of marketing to women available.

What Exactly is Word-of-Mouth Marketing?

The consumer is ultimately in control of WOM, because they control the message. But you CAN control the triggers, touch points, and vehicles by which you start WOM and make it easy to spread. So what are the different kinds of word-of-mouth marketing?

The Word of Mouth Marketing Association, WOMMA, lists the different types of word-of-mouth marketing. Here are some of the most common techniques.

- **Buzz Marketing:** Using high-profile entertainment or news to get people to talk about your brand.
- **Viral Marketing:** Creating entertaining or informative messages that are designed to be passed along in an exponential fashion, often electronically or by e-mail.
- **Community Marketing**: Forming or supporting niche communities that are likely to share interests about the brand (such as user groups, fan clubs, and discussion forums); providing tools, content, and information to support those communities.
- **Evangelist Marketing:** Cultivating evangelists, advocates, or volunteers who are encouraged to take a leadership role in actively spreading the word on your behalf.
- **Product Seeding:** Placing the right product into the right hands at the right time: providing information or samples to influential individuals.
- **Influencer Marketing:** Identifying key communities and opinion leaders who are likely to talk about products and have the ability to influence the opinions of others.

- **Cause Marketing:** Supporting social causes to earn respect and support from people who feel strongly about the cause.
- **Conversation Creation**: Interesting or fun advertising, e-mails, catch-phrases, entertainment, or promotion designed to start word-of-mouth activity.
- **Brand Blogging:** Creating blogs and participating in the blogosphere, in the spirit of open, transparent communications; sharing information of value that the blog community may talk about.
- **Referral Programs:** Creating tools that enable satisfied customers to refer their friends.

How to Buy Word of Mouth

Monday Morning Memo for October 31, 2005
by Roy H. Williams, the Wizard of Ads

The price of making a powerful statement is cheap compared to the cost of ads that don't work. So make a statement that counts. This is the best advice I can give you.

I'm not talking about making a grand and sweeping claim, such as, "Lowest prices anywhere. We won't be undersold." No one believes hype anymore. I'm talking about a statement that is bona fide, no loopholes, easy to experience. And it only takes one such statement to put a business over the top. This is why you should designate a percentage of your ad budget to purchase word-of-mouth advertising.

Word of mouth is credible because a person puts their reputation on the line every time they make a recommendation. And that person has nothing to gain but the appreciation of those who are listening. What are you doing to make sure your potential ambassadors feel secure? What are you doing to trigger word of mouth?

1. **Word of mouth is triggered** when a customer experiences something far beyond what was expected. Slightly exceeding their expectations just won't do it.

2. **Don't depend on your staff** to trigger word of mouth by delivering "exceptional customer service." Good service is expected. It's bad service we talk about. Great service can increase customer retention and generate lots of positive feedback to the business owner, but rarely is it the basis for word-of-mouth advertising.

3. **Physical, nonverbal statements** are the most dependable in triggering word of mouth. These statements can be architectural, kinetic, or generous, but they must go far beyond the boundaries of what is normal.

4. **BUDGET to DELIVER** the experience that will trigger word of mouth. Sometimes your word-of-mouth budget will be incremental, so that its cost is tied to your customer count. Other times it will require a capital investment, so that repayment will have to be withheld from your advertising budget over a period of years. The greatest danger isn't in overspending, but in under spending. Under spending for a word-of-mouth trigger is like buying a ticket halfway to Europe.

5. **Don't promise it in your ads**. Although it's tempting to promise the thing you're counting on to trigger word of mouth, these promises will only eliminate the possibility of your customer becoming your ambassador. Why would a customer repeat what you say about yourself in your ads? You must allow your customer to deliver the good news. Don't rob your ambassador of their moment in the sun.

Your word-of-mouth trigger can be **architectural**, **kinetic**, or **generous**.

1. **Architectural:** This can be product design, store design, fantasy décor, etc. The piano store that looks like a huge piano, with black and white keys forming the long awning over the long front porch. The erupting volcano outside the Mirage in Las Vegas. A glass-bottom floor that allows customers to see what's happening far below them. Do you remember when McDonalds began building playgrounds attached to all their restaurants? It worked like magic for twenty years.

2. **Kinetic:** Activity. Motion. "Performance" by every definition of the word. The tossing of fresh fish from one employee to another at Pike Place Market in Seattle (the inspiration for FISH!, that bestselling book, and training film). The magical, twirling knives of the tableside chefs at Benihana. Kissing the codfish when you get "screeched in" at any pub in Newfoundland. (A screech-in is a loud and funny ceremony where non-Newfoundlanders down a shot of cheap rum, repeat some phrases in the local dialect, and kiss a codfish. Everyone who visits that wonderful island returns home with a story of being "screeched in.") While it may at first seem like a staff-driven, kinetic word-of-mouth trigger is a violation of number 2 in the previous section, "Don't depend on your staff;" it's really not. A staff-driven kinetic word-of-mouth trigger is constantly observable by management. It isn't a "customer service" experience delivered privately, one on one. Extraordinary product performance is another kind of kinetic trigger. If a laundry detergent dramatically outperformed all others, its performance would likely become a kinetic word-of-mouth trigger. But remember, slightly exceeding customer expectations is usually not enough.

3. **Generous:** Extremely large portions in a diner. Oversized seats on an airplane. Are you willing to become known as the restaurant that allows its guests to select—at no charge—their choice of desserts from an expensive dessert menu? You can easily cover the hard cost of it in the prices of your entrees and drinks. Flour, butter, and sugar are cheap advertising. Are you the jewelry store that's willing to become known for replacing watch batteries at no charge, even when the customer hasn't purchased anything and didn't buy the watch from your store? Word will spread. And batteries cost less than advertising. Why sell them for a few lousy dollars when they're worth so much more as a word-of-mouth trigger?

Architectural, kinetic, generous: these are the flour, butter, and sugar of effective word of mouth. What can you make from these ingredients? Will you put their rich taste into the mouths of your potential word-of-mouth ambassadors? Or will you make ambiguous claims in your ads and hope that people are willing to believe them?

—Roy H. Williams

Why Is WOM So Powerful in Marketing to Women?

Why is word of mouth so powerful for women? Let's look at their deeper motivations. Why do women tell one another about products or services? They want to enhance their relationships and they want to enhance their reputations.

A woman values relationships more than almost anything else in her life. This is absolutely key for word-of-mouth marketers to understand. She will not do anything to jeopardize these relationships. She will not pass along information unless she truly trusts you and feels your product has a true benefit. If your company or product does not behave in a manner that she expects, if she's recommended you or your service to someone she has a relationship with and that person has a bad experience, there is going to be hell to pay. Because not only do you look bad; *she* looks bad. The trust between her and the person she made the recommendation to has been broken.

The only thing you can do that's worse than mistreating or disappointing her is to mistreat or disappoint someone she cares about. Women feel responsible. She may well feel her friend's bad experience is now her fault. And BOY does she hate that. Now she's dealing with the double whammy of anger and guilt. Bad. Very, very bad.

Women value their reputations. They work hard to gain confidences and trust. They want to be perceived as knowledgeable, reliable, and caring. If they discover something wonderful, they want to pass it along, not only because it will help people they care about (relationship), but it makes them look good (reputation).

Word of mouth is all about building relationships, reputations, or giving. No wonder word-of-mouth marketing and women are such a perfect fit.

If there is one thing to keep in mind when using word of mouth in marketing to women, you must be *ethical* and you must be *transparent.* Women despise anything unethical. Perhaps this is why so many whistleblowers are women. *Time* magazine featured three female corporate whistle-blowers as their "Persons of the Year."

Be transparent. We've talked about this before and cannot stress it enough. If you are actively promoting your product, let her know who you are and what your intentions are. If she feels like you have deceived or manipulated her, she will never forgive you.

So, when you're creating word-of-mouth marketing, keep these things in mind:

- **Be authentic and ethical**. Be upfront about who you are and what you're doing. Do not make her feel manipulated. Also, be careful of how you reward her for promoting your product. She may not feel right taking an incentive to promote your product if it feels like a pure "We'll pay you X if you do this for us." She does not want to feel bought. She does not want to feel like she's selling out her friends by giving you their e-mail addresses. Make sure you are upfront and explain clear value. Don't be pushy.

- **Be relevant**. Make sure what you're doing matters to her, let her know how it ties in with her life, needs, wants, desires. Make sure your word-of-mouth marketing effort ties in with a relevant aspect of your product. Creating a publicity stunt with live cows in Times Square might get you a lot of media coverage, but if you're selling baby products, it's not going to be relevant to your target audience.
- **Create a remarkable product**. Trying to take an unremarkable product and create a buzz is basically lying to your customer. It's hyping the product to be something it's not. Remember her bullshit detector. Your product must be worth talking about.
- **Be 100 percent accountable**. How you deal with negative WOM is almost more important than how you handle positive WOM (more on this later).
- **Listen.** Allow your customers to share their opinions with you; let them help craft your marketing message. No one knows better than they what really matters to them. You may want to promote your baby food as being healthy, but if women say they love it because their kids love the taste, you'd better include "Kids love the taste" in your marketing message.
- **Keep your promises.** Make sure your company and your product behave the way she expects. Don't disappoint her. If you can't live up to your claims, don't make them. Do NOT make her look bad.
- **Make it easy for her to pass along the message.** Don't make her fill out a long form, and don't ask for information about her friends. Provide a "Tell a friend" link so she can forward information with one click. Let her get her rebate with one e-mail rather than clipping the proof of purchase and having to physically mail it into you. Create a discussion forum and make it simple for her to post her opinion and see the opinions of others.
- **Exclusive access**. Provide a way for her and those she chooses to have exclusive access to something: A party, premier, "first to know" an announcement, or concert tickets before they go on sale to the public.

- **Provide value not only to the referrer but also to the referee**. Include an element where she gains AND the other person gains as well.

Let's explore this last point in more detail because it's so important. Let's say you want her to recommend to a friend that she try your product. You could give her an incentive: "Refer a friend and we'll give you $10 off your next purchase." But keep in mind she does not want to feel bought. Plus, she'd really like to pass along something special to her friend as well. A better, stronger offer would be "Refer a friend and we'll give you $10 off, *and* we'll give your friend $10 off." NOW you're talking. It enhances her reputation because she's turning her friend on to a product she has discovered. It enhances her relationship because her friend now gets something as well.

Not too long ago, a car company had a promotion where someone could win twelve cars. The commercials promoting the contest showed a guy with a huge trailer of cars going around town handing out keys to all his friends and family. The commercial could easily have featured a woman, as this is her most perfect dream.

Don't just give away a trip for two. Give away a trip for ten. Find a way to make her the hero. She will be more likely to spread your message if there is more value for her friends than for her.

Who Should Spread the Message: Finding Influencers

Besides creating a product worth talking about, the other most important thing you need to do is identify who the target audience is for your product. What user groups will benefit the most?

If you're selling baby products, identify the different groups that would be interested in or have contact with people who would use these products. You could focus on moms, pediatricians, day-care center operators, single moms, grandparents, and fathers.

Once you've identified the different groups, go even deeper. For example, if it's a product that saves time, target working mothers. You could target women business owners, networking groups for women in business, community colleges where adult women get business degrees, book clubs, etc.

Not to beat a dead horse, but remember this important point: *Understand your customer and how she lives her life.* Find out what her networks, groups, or "hives" are. Find out how you can provide something of value to them, something worth talking about and worth passing along.

Negative Word of Mouth

This is the single biggest fear of most companies when it comes to word of mouth. How do you control negative word of mouth? The answer is, you can't.

If someone posts a negative review or comment, you have to let it stay there. (And that's only in the cases where you can actually control the content.) Negative word of mouth can actually build credibility for your brand. If someone reads nothing but glowing reviews, she may be skeptical. If you allow people to share less than positive word of mouth, it makes it seem more real, more balanced.

The natural inclination is to jump in and debate the person, but that response isn't always prudent. A wonderful thing sometimes happens when you just sit back and let the discussion flow organically. Your supporters jump in and defend your position for you, which is way more powerful than you defending yourself. These quiet advocates often don't feel the need to speak up until someone starts bad-mouthing you. Negative word of mouth can actually encourage supporters you didn't even know you had.

That's the positive side. The negative side is that people are saying bad things about you. The best option is almost always to try to engage them on a one-to-one basis and attempt to fix the problem. Often the customers who sing your praises the loudest are those who had a complaint but then that complaint was handled promptly and the process exceeded their expectations. How you handle problems is absolutely key to how your company and brand will be perceived.

Make absolutely sure customers have a way to contact you with a problem, and that you provide a quick, satisfactory, or more than satisfactory, resolution. Women are tired of being ignored or made to feel like they are unimportant. Let them know they are important. Let them know just how much they and their business matters to you. If you handle the situation the right way, you'll not only regain a customer, you'll gain an advocate. Mishandle the situation, and she'll tell everyone she knows, and a few more people, just how upset she is.

Word of Mouth: Short-Term Versus Long-Term Strategy?

Word of mouth is a *short-term* strategy when you are truly just trying to create buzz about something, like an outrageous event, a quirky video, a downloadable coupon for free ice cream. The objective is to get attention or drive a short-term action. Our complaint about some of these strategies is they often don't tie in directly with the brand. (Think relevance.)

Look at Burger King's Subservient Chicken. There are a lot of different opinions as to whether it was successful or not. It depends on how you measure success. The website got over four hundred million views, but did it sell any food? If the strategy was to sell Burger King's new Tendercrisp Chicken Sandwiches, we're not sure what kind of an impact it made. If the strategy was to create something "hip and cool" that would then make people think Burger King was "hip and cool," there may be an argument there. Our biggest problem is there was little tie-in between the brand and the word-of-mouth marketing vehicle.

Word of mouth is a *long-term* strategy when you are trying to build a relationship with your customers and when the WOM is tied directly to the brand or brand attribute. Some examples could be a cookware maker creating cookbooks with recipes targeted at their customers, or software companies allowing employees to blog openly about what's going on and getting customer feedback on product development.

This is the true value of word of mouth in marketing to women, building relationships, relationships between her and her friends, relationships between her and your brand. It lets her become a participant instead of just a spectator.

Word-of-Mouth Example—Bad

Here's an example from an e-mail campaign from Audible.com.

Dear Holly,

Let Audible pay your bills! Tell your friends about us and you could win $1000!

Your friends and family would love to know about Audible's low prices and wide selection of audio programs. Tell one friend, and if he or she mentions your name when registering at audible.com, you will get one chance to win $1000.

- Refer one person and you'll earn one chance to win $1000.
- Refer 100 people, earn 100 chances.
- If someone you refer joins AudibleListener and remains a member for three months, you'll earn one free audiobook credit!
- If five people you refer join AudibleListener and remain members for three months, you'll earn five audiobook credits and a $50 audible.com gift certificate!

So what are you waiting for? Tell your friends about Audible's special 14-day trial membership today and you could win $1000 for your bills! Click the link below to learn more:

Hurry! This sweepstakes ends on November 3, 2005, 11:59 EST.

Best wishes,

The Audible Team

No purchase necessary. A purchase will not improve chances of winning. Odds of winning will vary based on the number of entries received. Please see Terms and Conditions on our website for further details.

Click here to forward this e-mail to a friend

What's missing? There's no benefit to the person I forward this to. Does my friend get a discount? Does she get a chance to win money?

Also, the only copy that addresses the "benefits" you pass along for forwarding (benefits to the recipient) are "low prices and wide selection of audio programs." More text focusing on how your friends can benefit would really strengthen this offer. (Audible.com offers a fabulous service.) What if the e-mail included text like this: "What do you love most about Audible? How easy it is to use, instant access, all the money you save? Would you friends value that as well? Have friends that love to read but never have time? Have friends spending $30, $40, or even more on books-on-tape or books-on-CD? Would they like to be able to access all their favorite titles instantly for as little as $XX per audiobook?"

How much stronger would this call to action be for women if they could not only see the benefit for themselves but also the benefit for their friends? Plus, Audible would be reinforcing their brand by reminding their members why they love Audible. This is a much stronger tie to the brand than simply giving away a chance to win cash.

Word of Mouth Example—Good

Meet Coco, a fifteen-year-old Bichon Frise who really doesn't like anyone except her immediate family. Coco hates, and we do mean *hates,* going to the groomer. That is, until her mom tried a new groomer in the area called Beach Paws.

When Coco's mom went to pick up her freshly coiffed pooch, she was met with quite a surprise. Normally, Coco would have run frantically to her, shaking, and doing everything she could to make her mom feel guilty for putting her through such a traumatic experience.

This time, however, Coco was not shaking. Coco did not go running to her mother. As a matter of fact, Coco was completely ignoring her mother, contentedly walking around, and only occasionally glancing in her mom's direction with a look of "Who are you?"

Why was this experience at the groomer so much better than previous ones? The groomer explained that they use a special oatmeal scrub on the dogs, especially ones with sensitive skin like Coco's. While Coco had been nervous at first, once she sensed how good that oatmeal scrub felt, she was a persuaded pooch.

They say dogs are like their owners, so no one was surprised when Coco's mother, a woman who actually attempted "*death by spa,*" announced that her canine would become a Beach Paws frequent customer. She spread the oatmeal scrub story and sent several other puppy parents to Beach Paws.

This kind of unexpected surprise is what Roy H. Williams, author of the best-selling *Wizards of Ads* trilogy, refers to as *lagniappe*, a term that comes from southern Louisiana and Mississippi. It means "the offering of a little something extra, an unexpected gift or benefit." It's a great catalyst for word of mouth.

Have you ever gone to the butcher and had him throw in an extra lamb chop or give you an extra quarter pound of ground meat for free? That's lagniappe, or in this case, "lamb-iappe."

Conclusion

Word-of-mouth marketing is a huge opportunity to spread your message quickly and cheaply. But you must be remarkable. Creating hype for hype's sake will not provide lasting results. Word-of-mouth marketing is a natural for women. They love to help their friends and turn them on to wonderful new companies, services, and products. So, in the words of Bonnie Raitt, "*Let's give them something to talk about.*"

19

Blogs:

The Deeper Online Connection

The word blogs, besides just being fun to say, is a word we're hearing a lot about these days. Blogs are a very important new vehicle for marketing. But why is so much attention being paid to blogs? And what the heck are they anyway?

The word blog is short for web log, a frequently updated web-based journal that's intended for general public consumption. Blogs consist of posts, short entries that are updated and listed chronologically.

According to the blog tracking firm Technorati, there are currently fourteen million blogs, with eighty thousand more being added every day. And 30 percent of all fifty million Internet users are blog readers. In short, a lot of people are reading and writing blogs.

Blogs usually fall into two general categories:

- **Personal blogs**: a mixture of a personal diary, opinion posts, and research links
- **Business blogs**: a corporate tool for communicating with customers or employees to share knowledge and expertise

Business Blogs

For our purposes, we're going to focus on business blogs. Why are blogs important to businesses?

- Business blogs are a wonderful way to communicate and connect with current and potential customers.
- It's a way for consumers to get to know the blogger (blog author), whether that's the company owner, CEO, or an employee.
- Blogs are very cost-effective. It costs next to nothing to set up and maintain a blog. But beware, blogs do require a certain time commitment.
- You can distribute breaking news and information quickly. It takes only minutes to put up a new post. It takes much longer, and is much more work, to get the information up on your regular website.
- Blogs are great for search engine optimization. Blog posts can be keyword and link rich, both of which search engines love. Each individual blog entry exists as a separate page that can also be picked up by the search engines. And as your blog grows, you'll also have blog archive pages that will also exist separately. Blog directories and RSS feed directories provide even more opportunities for visitors to find your blog and thus your information.
- Blogs have a natural viral quality. It's easy for your content to get picked up by other blogs and websites. In other words, it's a great way to spread your message and ideas.
- Blogs allow you to get instant feedback from your customers. Blogs give you the option of accepting comments. If you do, you provide a simple, quick way for your customers to share their opinions.
- Blogs allow you to display your knowledge of a product or subject. Especially if you are in a services industry, a blog can be the perfect vehicle to build your reputation as an expert in your field.
- RSS feeds allow visitors to sign up to receive all your new posts automatically. This allows you to bypass the problems of e-mail and e-mail filtering. And best yet, these RSS feeds cost you nothing.

Using Blogs to Market to Women

Why are blogs the perfect vehicle for marketing to women? We've listed some of the reasons previously; and here are a few more:

- Blogs tend to be more personal. They have a more informal voice than most websites. Blog authors often share more personal information, so you can really get to know the blogger.
- Blogs are interactive and create a sense of community. Readers can post and read comments from other readers. This allows women to take part in the discussion and share their view as well as seeing the views of others.
- Blogs don't require you to be technically savvy. Most blog software is designed to be extremely user-friendly. Almost anyone can set up and use a blog. Some of the most popular choices are Typepad and WordPress.
- Blogs create relationships, relationships between the reader and the blogger, and between other bloggers interested in the same field or topic. Blogs allow women to find other people with similar interests. They allow you to find your tribe.
- Blogs have a natural viral quality. Thanks to permalinks, trackbacks, etc. blogs link back and forth between one another. That makes it easy to get a wide variety of opinions on products, services, or companies you're interested in.
- Blogs allow you to be an expert in your field. This allows women, who need to build trust before they buy, to get to know you in a no-pressure situation. People can determine from your writing if your knowledge and style are right to solve their problems. When you give helpful free advice, readers will likely have a more positive impression of you.

Jory Des Jardins is one of the founders of BlogHer, the world's number one company by, for, and about women bloggers (http://blogher.com). Jory has this insight into why blogging is a natural for women:

> *Women are referrers, and the blogging ethic requires people to not be islands unto themselves if they are to gain any traction in the blogosphere. I'm sure there are people out there who just write and never link or reach out and still manage to enjoy some degree of traffic. But for the typical blogger, you must refer, provide suggestions, and interact in order to maintain a readership. Women are naturals at this. By nature we make others feel heard, we empathize, we tell stories (another piece of the blogging ethic), we love to tell our friends and community about the great find/sale/resource we've uncovered.*
>
> *I realize this isn't exclusive to women, but it isn't as natural to men. One of the main characteristics of women is our innate desire to share. If someone compliments a man on his jacket, he says, "thanks." Compliment a woman, and she says, "Thanks! You know, I had to stand in line at J. Crew for an hour to buy it, but I had this wedding to go to and was desperate for something in black. I almost didn't get it." You get the point.*
>
> —Jory Des Jardins BlogHer, Inc.

Personal or Business

Some business bloggers struggle with the choice between providing personal information and entertainment, OR providing valuable content with solid educational value. If you look at Michele Miller's and Holly Buchanan's blogs, you'll see that we tend to fall somewhere in the middle. We both provide some personal anecdotes from our daily lives. But we also try to follow that up with some sort of useful information that provides genuine value to the reader.

Bottom line: If you provide valuable insight for your reader, and can do it in an entertaining and personal way, chances are you'll have a successful blog.

Real-Life Examples

Michele Miller's blog: www.michelemiller.blogs.com. Here are some things Michele does to make her blog successful:

- Images in each post. Michele does a wonderful job of including images that add a visually interesting element to almost every post.

- Links from her blog to her website, and from her website to her blog.
- A fantastic video you can watch (well worth it). You'll get a real idea of who Michele is.
- The comments feature is enabled so visitors can share their opinions.
- RSS feed sign-up.
- Listing of other interesting blogs and websites she recommends.

This last feature is really important. Surf the Internet and find other blogs that interest you. They can be on the same subject, related subjects, or even unrelated subjects. Include links to their blogs. You can approach them and see if they will link to your blog as well, but don't make it mandatory. If you like someone else's work, link to it even if they don't provide a reciprocal link back to you.

Holly Buchanan's blogs: Grokdotcom.com/women and marketingtowomen online.typepad.com. (NOTE: marketingtowomenonline.com is a different site belonging to the fabulous Yvonne DiVita. If you want Holly's blog, make sure you add "typepad.com")

Here are some things Holly does to make her blogs successful:

- **Keyword rich posts.** Research the keywords which might be used by visitors interested in your content and include those keywords in your posts.
- **Keyword rich categories**. It's important to have a focus for your blog, but then break down the different subcategories of that focus. When you create posts, you can list them in the appropriate category. Example: If someone were searching for information on stereotypes of women in the media, they could go to that category in Holly's blog and find lots of posts on that particular subject.
- **"Tip" rich copy**. You'll find a lot of "10 tips to . . ." or "5 tips to . . ." This "how to" copy is great for business owners looking for something to take away or a post they can link to that will provide value for themselves or their readers.
- **Contact information**. Even if you don't have a website to link to, make sure you include a bio of who you are and an e-mail address. For security reasons, we do NOT recommend you put phone numbers, addresses, or other personal information in your contact information.

- **Blog name and URL that reflects the information on your blog.** Remember, many blogs are listed by their title. If your blog name is "Susan's Blog," no one will know what the subject matter is and will not likely take the time to click through to find out. "Marketing to Women Online" lets people know exactly what subject matter the blog focuses on

If you're looking for a marketing vehicle that costs you next to nothing, blogs are a great way to go to get your message out. Just make sure you're willing to make the time commitment to keep it updated and interesting. Isn't it time you joined the blogosphere?

Tips for Creating a Successful Blog

What else can you do to make your blog successful? Here are some tips from John Jantsch, author of *Duct Tape Marketing: The World's Most Practical Small Business Marketing Guide* and his own blog www.ducttapemarketing.com/blog.

- Post almost daily—keep at it for months.
- Answer the questions your clients ask you in your posts.
- Promote the heck out of your blog online and offline.
- Build a network of users and connectors around your blog.
- Read and participate in other blogs almost daily.
- Integrate your blog into your website, ezine, and marketing materials.
- Update the non-post elements of your blog frequently.

Conclusion

The future of marketing is changing. You can't keep doing things the way you used to and expect the same kinds of returns. But there are some exciting new opportunities including, but not limited to, the Internet, word-of-mouth advertising, and blogs. But these mediums are a perfect fit with women. In the next chapters we'll discuss how women and men approach the Internet differently. How can you create a website that serves your female customers and meets all their needs? Let's take a look.

Websites for Women:

How to Create a Website for Your Female Customers

Why Do Women Shop Online?

Do women shop the same way online as they shop offline? Do they have the same needs, questions, buying process? Is it true that what's most important to them offline is also what's most important to them online?

There is something unique about actually being in a store, feeling, touching, trying on, getting new ideas. There's something about that environment that women truly enjoy.

So, if the women who truly love the shopping experience shop online instead of offline, there is usually a reason for it. There is something that the online experience offers that the offline does not. There is a reason why she is on the Internet and not in a store.

What are the main reasons women shop online?

- **To save time**. She doesn't have to drive all over to find what she wants. And she can shop on her schedule.

- **To get a better selection**. She wants more choice and a way to find exactly what she wants, in an exact model, size, and color.
- **To research a product**. She wants to get all her questions answered so she can make a more educated decision.
- **To get a better value**. This can mean a lower price, superior service, or added value, like free shipping.
- **Anonymity**. She may be shopping for a more private item, or may simply not want to be judged or condescended to.
- **Logistics**. For example, if there isn't a branch of the store near her, and she's buying a gift, then it's easier to buy and send online than buy offline and have to wrap it and go to the post office.

Because of these factors, women are shopping online in ever-increasing numbers. As we've said before, the Internet is a perfect fit in women's lives today. And keep in mind that she may start her buying process online and purchase offline. So even if you're not actually selling products online, it's still important to have an Internet presence so you make it onto her radar screen and have a voice in her decision process.

How Women Use the Internet Versus Men

Do women use the Internet differently than men do? Yes, say several studies. According to a report from the Pew Internet & American Life Project, *How Women and Men Use the Internet*, Deborah Fallows, December 28, 2005, there are definite differences in how women and men use the Internet. Here are some interesting findings:

- **Young women are more likely to be online than young men, and black women have surged online** in the last three years. Want to reach younger women and minority women? The Internet's an increasingly good place to find them.
- **Sixty-five percent of men and 66 percent of women use the Internet at work**. Keep this in mind when you build your websites with flash and streaming video that launch automatically. Imagine

her horror if she lands on your website and before she can click out of your site or hit the volume button, "Welcome to XYZ cosmetics, where all your fantasies come true" or some similar sales message comes blaring from her computer, alerting every last one of her co-workers that she is shopping online when she should be working.

- **Women are using search engines but are not as confident with the results they find**. Ninety percent of men and women who go online use search engines. Men and women generally use the same kinds of search strategies. But men are a lot more confident in themselves as searchers. Women seem more overwhelmed by the volume of information around them. Whether you're targeting keywords, doing a PPC campaign, or designing landing pages, make sure they are relevant and consistent. If your PPC ad is targeting "cloth versus disposable baby diapers," make sure it takes her to a landing page with a clear header and content that discusses cloth versus disposable diapers (as opposed to just promoting your disposable baby diapers, with no mention of her desire to compare them to cloth diapers).
- **The proportion of Internet users who have participated in online chats and discussion groups dropped from 28 percent in 2000 to as low as 17 percent in 2005, entirely because of the falloff in women's participation**. Women can harbor more fears about online risks and dangers than men, from privacy to criminal activity. So, do everything you can to assure her that her information will be kept private and secure right at the point where you ask her to give you that information. Monitor your chat rooms and let her know what steps you take to keep her safe.
- **More men have high-speed Internet access than women**. There are still quite a few women out there using dial-up connections. How quickly do your pages load for a 56K modem? Have you carefully sized your images for quicker loading time? Do your pages include a lot of flash and fancy graphics that take a long time to load? Reduce your page sizes and always test your load times.
- **Eighty-two percent of men and 75 percent of women research products and services**. Women are catching up to men quickly, with

an increase in this category of 3 percent for men versus 12 percent for women. Are you answering all her questions about your product and service? Are you going beyond spec sheets and clearly spelling out all the benefits to her?

- **Women are online in increasing numbers to seek advice from family and friends**. So tap into the power of word-of-mouth advertising. Find new ways to help her talk about and recommend you and your products and services.
- **Women value e-mail in the workplace**. Thirty-two percent of men think e-mail is most effective for asking questions, while 39 percent of women value it for this reason. Once again, women are looking for a safe environment in which to ask questions. Does your online presence answer her questions? Do you even know what questions she is asking?
- **When shopping online, more men than women value cost savings**. Thirty-five percent of men want to save money, while only 28 percent of women say saving money is why they shop online. So, while cost may not be at the top of her list, value is. Find ways to show her the value of what you offer. (Think free shipping.) The lowest price isn't always the best way to get her business.
- **Women appreciate shopping online to find unusual gifts more than men do**. No surprise, since women are big gift givers. Do you make it easy for her to send a gift? Do you include clear gift options? Do you offer gift wrapping and gift messaging?
- **More men search the Internet for fun, while women have a specific purpose**. This is interesting because a widely held belief is that just the opposite is true; that men are more task-oriented while women enjoy browsing around. But it's been our experience that, when using the Internet, women are usually more task oriented. So, make it easy for her to find exactly what she's looking for with clear navigation, intuitive categories, and clear calls to action. If she doesn't find exactly what she's looking for, she will more likely leave and search somewhere else rather than settle for "close enough."

Let's take a closer look at this last point, since it's so important. On the Internet, women can be just as task-oriented as men, if not more task-oriented. Women's number one complaint is that they don't have enough time. They love the Internet because it saves them time.

Remember, women were slower to take up the Internet largely due to usability issues. They're jumping aboard in record numbers largely because the Internet has become much more user-friendly. Men are famous for not asking directions; they'll just feel their way around. Women want to know where they're going. They want a clear map to help them get from their starting point to their destination. I'd argue that the same is true with the Internet. If a woman has to guess about non-obvious navigation, your site is going to lose trust and credibility.

As for the browsing thing, don't confuse online shopping with offline shopping. Offline she may browse for hours through stores, especially when buying clothes. But online, she is trying to save time; she has a purpose. If she is early in the buying process, she may search through different sites, educating herself and getting ideas. But she still has a specific purpose or task. She's not just browsing for the heck of it. She wants to buy a new pair of black designer heels. She wants to get a new cell phone with better coverage. She wants to know what treatments are available for her husband's newly diagnosed health problem. Is she really going to explore every nook and cranny of the website? ONLY if it clearly provides information that is relevant to what she is searching for. Otherwise, she does not have time.

The Importance of Categorization and Filtering Options

Take a close look at your categorization. Women may categorize products differently than men do. They may have different criteria they use to narrow down their choices.

Take clothing: Categories like "shirts" and "dresses" often aren't enough. Women think of big-picture categories and how they might use a product like "summer cocktail outfits."

Look at shoes. DesignerShoes.com lets her sort by things like heel size. How cool is that? They also have categories like "bridal/dyeable." They know that when you're trying to find shoes to wear with a bridesmaid's dress, you often need to dye shoes to match. Other categories include "comfortable" for women who are on their feet all day and "vegan" for women who don't wear animal products.

Take a wine website. Go beyond the usual choices of red, white, region, or price. She might want to know "what goes great with pork" or benefit from a useful suggestion such as: "If you like Fat Bastard Chardonnay you may also like the following Chardonnays." (If you haven't tried Fat Bastard Chardonnay, you really should. It's just plain fun to order.)

It's vitally important to provide more and better ways to help her find exactly what she needs by using categories and "sort by" options that help her instantly narrow down her search based on the criteria that is most important to her.

Product Reviews

Product reviews are increasingly important for all buyers, but they are especially powerful with women for three reasons:

- **Trusted recommendations**. Because of their community nature, women often trust other consumers as their main source for product information and reviews.
- **More detailed product information**. Customer reviews often give more information about how a product is used and what the actual experience is like. Reviews are a great place for women, who often have more questions, to get those questions answered. Often, you'll find information in product reviews not addressed in manufacturer product descriptions.
- **Sorting functionality**. More and more websites allow you to sort by most highly rated product. This makes it easy for her to find products she knows will meet her often higher standards.

Bazaarvoice is a company specializing in helping websites set up customer ratings. Here are some stats they've gathered about the impact of customer reviews:

- RoperASW reports that the percentage who value of word of mouth as the best source of information on products has exploded from 67 percent in 1977 to 93 percent in 2001.
- BizRate found that 59 percent of their users considered customer reviews to be more valuable than expert reviews.
- Marketing Experiments Journal tested product conversion with and without product ratings by customers. Conversion nearly doubled, going from .44 percent to 1.04 percent after the same product displayed its five-star rating from customers.

These reviews can be a key source of information for all your visitors, but they are especially important to women.

Who Should Design Your Site: A Man or a Woman?

A 2005 study at the University of Glamorgan, in the United Kingdom, by Glora Moss and Dr. Rod Gunn, found that the sexes reacted very differently to sites when surfing the Internet.

The study found members of each sex preferred websites designed by their own sex. Not a big surprise, since web designers can sometimes design what *they* like, as opposed to what's truly best for their audience.

Nevertheless, a study of websites of thirty-two higher education institutions showed that 94 percent displayed a masculine orientation and just 2 percent a female bias. This was the case, even though all the schools' target audiences were almost equally balanced between the sexes.

The report also found that where visuals are concerned:

- Males favor the use of straight lines (as opposed to the rounded forms preferred by females).
- Males prefer few colors in the typeface and background.
- Males prefer formal typography.

As for language:

- Males favor the use of formal or expert language with few abbreviations and are more likely to promote themselves and their abilities heavily.

So, if you're designing a site for women consider:

- More rounded design
- Less formal typography, but make sure it is readable; that's the most important thing
- More conversational language with less thumping on the chest "W*e are this; we are that; we've got a hundred year history of this and that.*" More "you" language will resonate with her and help you build rapport. (This does not mean she does not want to know your credentials, she does, but she wants to know how those credentials are a benefit to her.)
- Color is a tricky area. We would not recommend throwing in lots and lots of color. She will appreciate a clean, usable design that is not too busy. More on that later.

Example: Female-oriented design

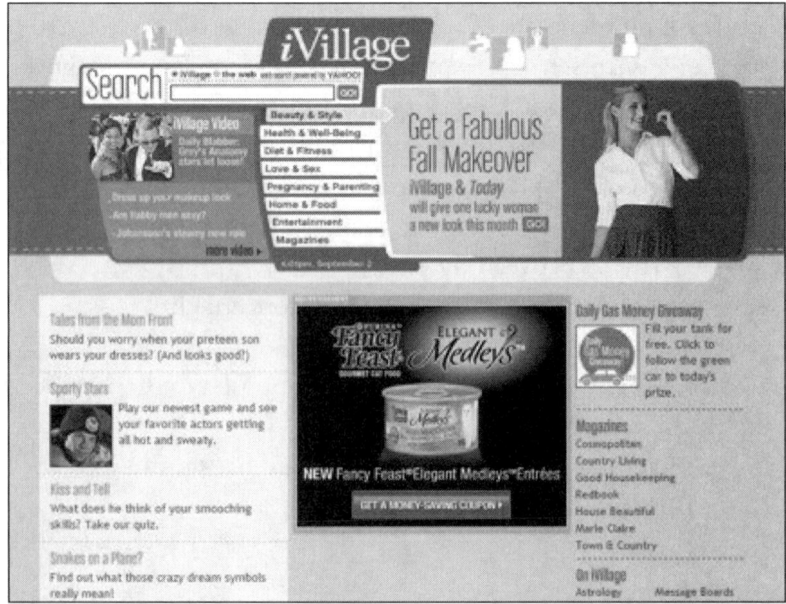

Example: Male-oriented design

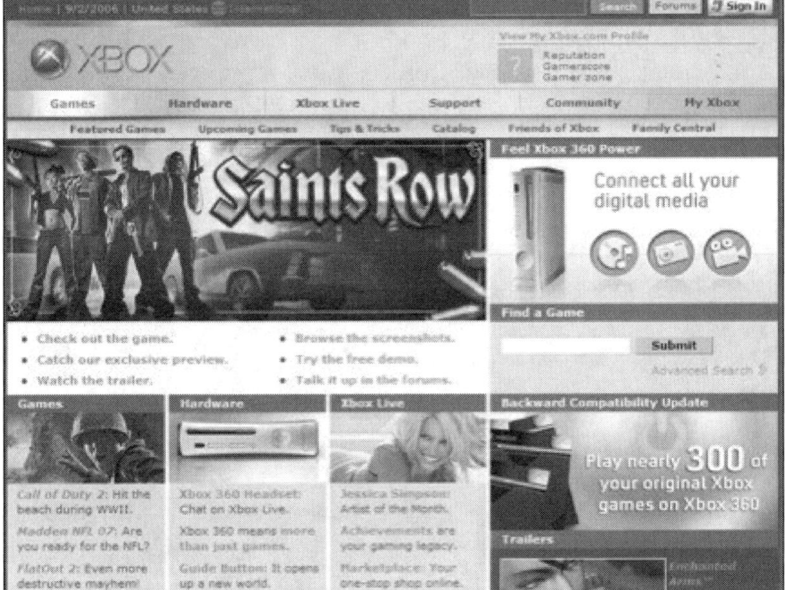

There are some definite aesthetic differences. This all begs the question of whether or not you should design your website differently for men than for women. Note: When I say design websites, I'm talking about more than just the template; I'm talking about navigation, usability, content, copy, etc.

The answer is yes, but with a caveat.

Your website should reflect who you are as a company. If you truly are female-focused and want to relay that to her, design your site with aesthetics women appreciate.

But what if you're appealing to both women and men? Then choose a design that once again reflects who you are as a company. If you are a bold, aggressive stockbroker, then you should consider a more masculine design that reflects that. If you are a counselor who specializes in dealing with personal issues, then you should consider a more feminine design that reflects who you are.

Now, should you hire a web designer based on the person's gender? Our answer is "No." Hire the best Web designer you can, regardless of gender. Really good Web designers should be empathetic and should be able to design a site that accurately represents who you are. Just make sure personal preferences don't creep in. If a designer really likes a certain design, he or she should be able to describe why they like it. That explanation should include specifics on how the design works for the target audience.

One final note: Please, please, Puhleeeeese . . . do not think adding cute wallpaper behind your design will make it more "female-friendly." Take a look at this example and you'll understand:

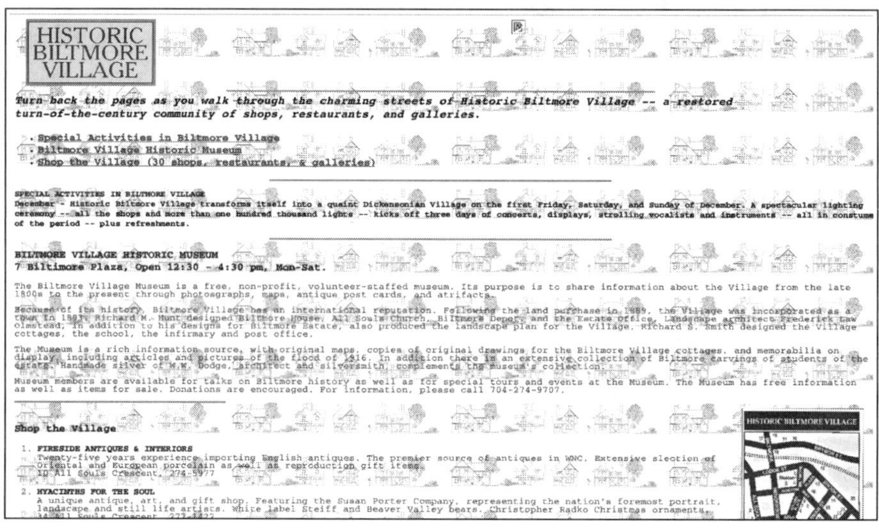

This busy background wallpaper makes the copy virtually impossible to read. If she can't read the copy, she can't interact with your website.

Conclusion

We are just now starting to understand the differences in how women and men use the Internet. We're sure many more studies will be coming out in the future that more thoroughly explore these differences.

But for now, focus in on the differences that have been observed to make sure you are meeting the needs of your female customers as well as your male ones. Because, as you'll see in the following chapter, improving the experience for women may actually improve the experience for men as well.

21

Gender Savvy:

How to Market to Women Without Alienating Men

There is no such thing as marketing to women. Go ahead, take a minute to get your wind back. We'll wait. OK, so we exaggerated just a bit but really only to make a very important point.

Marketing to women does exist, but always remember that *effective marketing to women never excludes men.* Connecting with women requires different marketing methods from what's traditionally been done but when done the right way, you also appeal to men.

Fundamentally, women are more demanding. By virtue of wiring in the brain, they typically have more questions than men . . . and require more of a sense of consensus. Successfully marketing to women depends on your ability to persuade a consumer to buy your product or service based on your understanding of human behavior, the different buying modes of consumers, and the universe of emotion, memory, and imagination that resides in the right hemisphere of the brain.

But men have a right brain, too, correct?

We're going to go out on the skinny part of the branch here and say that when it comes to marketing, the gender divide that many experts talk about (and we've touched on in this book) is actually less dramatic (or traumatic, depending on your perspective) than you might think. Yes, women have four times as many connections between the left and right hemispheres of the brain. All that really means is that women do three things much faster than men do: process information, determine recognizable patterns that are meaningful to them, and either connect or disconnect from your message much faster than men do.

Men *also* tap into emotion, memory, and imagination and they, too, have the ability to detect and link to patterns embedded in the right brain—just not at the same rate. No matter where society stands on the "nature versus nurture" debate, men *do* have needs and deeper motivations for connection, community, and beauty. And those needs and motivations are surprisingly similar to those of women (especially as men get older, according to brain researchers). That is the essence of phenomenally successful marketing strategies like those created by Lincoln Financial Group and Volvo: They approached the marketing of their products and services from a woman's perspective, knowing men wouldn't be far behind.

Women Buy Electronics—Men Buy Granite Countertops

We talked earlier about the Logitech Quick Cam example where Logitech recognized that women were buying their technology products as well as men. There is often a pervading view that technology products appeal only to men.

The same is true of many product categories where the pervading view is that only women buy these types of products. Take kitchen remodeling. Many manufacturers think the kitchen is the domain of the woman in the family. Not true. Here's a real-life example from Michele.

MICHELE: My husband and I recently decided to upgrade our kitchen countertops, replacing the Corian with slab granite. The project has grown in scale in proportion to The Money Pit. The domino effect takes your breath away. New countertops also mean a new sink, new faucet (and trappings), new cooktop, and everything else that trickles down from there.

I called home the other day from Austin and heard my husband declare, "We've decided to put tile up the walls for backsplash." Since I didn't remember discussing the topic, I presumed he meant either the royal "we" or a prearranged agreement with the dog. Whichever the case, it was fine with me. I am blessed with an artist for a husband, a man with impeccable taste. While we work as a team on projects like this, I have no qualms about having him choose every element—the result is guaranteed to be gorgeous.

Catching up by phone the next day, I was surprised to find a frustrated and despondent husband. "They wouldn't sell me any tile."

"What do you mean, *they wouldn't sell you any tile?*"

"Just what I said—the salesman ignored me. Then, he did everything to put obstacles in the way—said I had to hire someone to measure the kitchen, even though I had meticulous measurements with me. I even told him I'd pay extra to order enough tile to cover breakage *and* to have their guy come out and measure. All I wanted to do was order the f*****g tile, and he wouldn't let me! Then, when I asked him another question, he walked away from me—went over to a lady who was staring at tile samples."

By now, I was starting to get PO'd myself, but then I stopped. "You know why—besides being a jerk—this guy didn't sell you tile, don't you?"

"Why?"

"Because you were by yourself."

I could picture it: My husband wheeling his shopping cart around the store, transporting the cabinet door he takes with him everywhere to compare samples. I'm willing to bet he started the conversation by saying, "My wife and I are redoing our kitchen . . ."

From there, he was screwed.

Looking back at our other encounters during this project, I remembered being struck by the fact that sales reps often assumed I was making all the decisions, that my husband was a decorating dolt and was just along for the ride. Were they nice to him? Absolutely. But did they take him seriously? Most of the time, no. It was rather surreal—kind of like watching a car-buying experience in reverse.

It's also a rotten way to market to women. You see, women don't live in a vacuum. Often, a woman's loyalty to a brand stems from the way the people selling that brand treat the people around her, *not just her.* I love my husband and am protective of him; therefore, I take umbrage at the way any salesperson treats him.

The Fine Line:
Meet Her Needs, but Don't Alienate Him

There are some very real elements of marketing that must be approached from a unique angle when targeting women. Women do have massive purchasing power today and are saying, "Market to me as an individual, with specific needs and motivations." What they actually mean is "Talk to me with the respect and understanding I deserve, just like you've talked to men all these years."

The techniques presented in this book have been introduced to you through the platform of marketing to women because it's simply the easiest and most efficient way to create a powerful and profitable marketing campaign. If you can understand how to speak to women in a genuine, authentic way that persuades her to not only do business with you but also become a brand champion, you will find that men follow. Remember what Hans-Olov Olsson, the CEO of Volvo, said? "We learned that if you meet women's needs and expectations, you also exceed those for men."

The Third Wave era of marketing is first about marketing to women and second, about marketing to the right hemisphere of the brain that resides in each of us—the part that's touched by powerful words and extraordinary experience. Look at the topics we've covered in this book:

- Understanding basic gender differences.
- Shattering stereotypes.
- Creating personas and scenarios.
- Conducting research from "the inside out."
- Finding a voice and message that resonates.
- Recognizing trends in society and technology for the future.

Can the knowledge and principles you've gathered from the chapters in this book be applied to men as well as women? Of course they can. Both women *and* men are stereotyped in the marketing and advertising world, which accounts for the never-ending stream of ads and strategies that simply aren't relevant to your audience. You can create a set of personas that includes both women *and* men and reflects real-life buying scenarios.

Research methodologies like the ones we described in Chapter 11 are astoundingly effective with men as well as women. Best Buy made that discovery early on. After the eye-opening information that was revealed during the women's "conversation groups," Best Buy went on to duplicate the sessions using men, to enormous success. The company now has in-depth insight into people lives, wants, and needs that they otherwise might have missed, and can work to deliver just that through advertising, marketing, and the Internet.

Lite 101.5 FM:
Giving New Meaning to Having a Lite Day

When it comes to tuning in, more women listen to Miami's Lite 101.5 FM than any other station in southern Florida. It's no accident that Lite Miami has claimed either the number one or number two spot in radio ratings for more than fifteen years. Under the guidance of vice president Dennis Collins and program director Rob Sidney, the station has made a concerted effort to understand the needs of female listeners and has gone above and beyond in delivering the content that women love.

In the mid-1990s, the core of Lite Miami's message was "a place to come for stress relief." Smooth jazz and soft pop vocals were programmed to "soothe the soul," and every spoke in their Wheel of Persuasion, print materials, website, on-air announcements, and community outreach related directly to the hub of their message. For years, the station has experienced great success and is a beloved part of the Miami community. But recently, the staff sensed the need to reevaluate their direction. Utilizing online survey and conversation-group research methods, they detected a trend: Stress still exists, but women don't necessarily want to be reminded of it every minute of the day. In fact, there are even some women who *love* stress!

At first, the staff was perplexed. If women were moving away from needing constant stress relief, why was Lite Miami still such a popular station? They evaluated every spoke on their Wheel of Persuasion and discovered two things:

- One, they were doing many things right—things that shouldn't be changed, including their core message.

- Two, they originally had only one woman in mind as they created their marketing and programming strategy, when, in fact, they should have actually had four (to match the buying modes).

Keeping the core message of stress relief, Lite Miami developed four female personas to help them understand who they are talking to and what those personas need. Without changing the music format, they still talk about stress relief, but from different angles of approach. In one announcement, the on-air personality may say, "Soothing music for the quiet moments in your life." Later in the hour, the same personality may introduce a song, saying, "Here's a song to pump up your energy and help conquer the day ahead!" Same message, different dialect. Applying those dialects to everything from website to contests means Lite Miami will hold the number one position for many years to come, something that businesses which advertise on the station love to hear.

As only visionary companies do, Lite Miami then looked beyond the four buying modes and made a brilliant move. They developed a fifth persona—*a male listener.* Through research and word-of-mouth anecdotes, Lite Miami learned that the station is very popular with a certain segment of males in the region, many of whom spend a great deal of time in a vehicle as part of their job. The station is now working hard to acknowledge this male listener, which can only strengthen the connection with female listeners as well. For example, what used to be a focus on women's health issues now also includes men's health issues; segments on prostate screening, colonoscopies, etc. are now part of the typical programming day. Male listeners feel included, and female listeners (as the major decision makers when it comes to medical needs) love the fact that the station includes the whole family. Lite Miami is saying, "We recognize you in the context of your whole world."

Lite Miami is one of the rare companies that not only delves deep into understanding female consumers; it also recognizes that constant reevaluation of strategy is required, and that when done correctly, it attracts men as well.

How Do You Market to Women Online *Without Alienating Men Online?*

Men and women use the Internet as a research tool. Answer all of her many questions, and you'll probably answer his as well. Provide more detailed product descriptions that focus on benefits rather than features. Both men and women want to picture themselves using the product and understand how it can improve their lives. Be a trusted resource using conversational language and lifestyle images. While she may view the lifestyle image first, then be drawn to the product, he may be drawn to the product, then the image. But the combination of the two provides powerful persuasion.

Bottom line: If women want and expect more, then meeting their needs should raise the bar for your product or service. Providing a better product or service will please all your customers.

Home Improvement Stores: *Strong Enough for a Man, Made for a Woman*

Almost all of the big name home improvement stores have recognized the need to reach out to their female customers. An increasing number of women are homeowners and responsible for home maintenance. They have a lot of basic questions. They are working on home improvement projects. But are there men out there looking for this information as well? You bet. Some guys grow up with a great deal of knowledge about tools, repair, and maintenance. But some guys don't. Would they like to know home maintenance schedules, how to choose a repairman, and how to fix a faucet? Of course.

Be Jane has home improvement ideas geared toward women. They have clear simple explanations and a can-do attitude.

Could men benefit from clear simple explanations? Would they enjoy a supportive can-do attitude? Sure they would. Heidi Baker, Chief Jane Officer at Be Jane stresses that men are very welcome.

> *While we are here to empower women to take on home improvement projects, it is most certainly not exclusionary of men. We have found*

that the men who come to our site also enjoy it as we don't talk down to the reader and it's a safe place to land. Our goal is to try to empower them (male or female) into believing that they can take on the project at hand, be successful, and create a home they love to live in. Regardless of what your gender is, the first time you take on a specific project in home improvement, it can be rather daunting and down right scary so knowing you have a resource and community to chat with while you're going through the process is always a help.

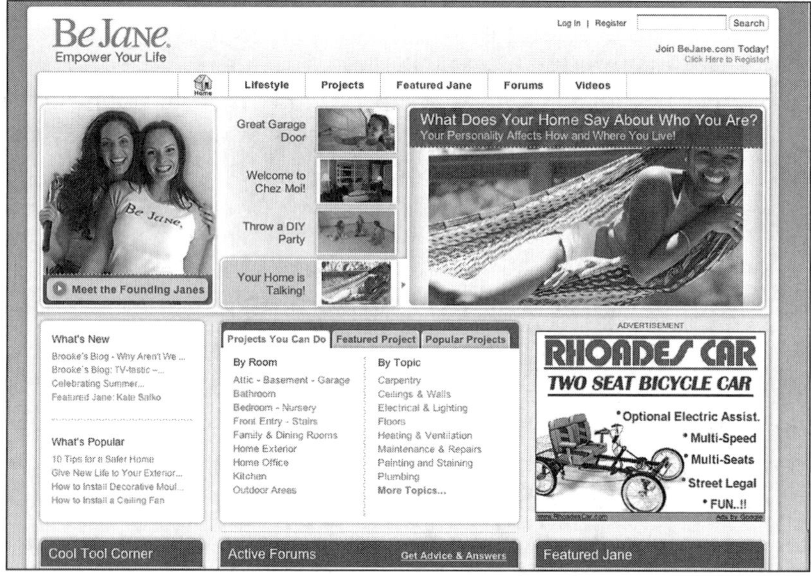

Other Ways Men Can Benefit
From an Experience Designed for Women

When designing a website for women, you need to have strong calls to action in the active window. They're looking for obvious directions. They don't want to just "click their way around" and hope they'll get where they're going. You're going to have to build very clear pathways. Will male visitors benefit from that as well? Yes, they will.

Women are very task-oriented when they're on the Internet. If they're looking for something specific, they won't stop until they find it. Close enough is not good enough. You're going to have to provide very clear categories. You're going to have to provide multiple categories that match the way she thinks of your product. Will men benefit from better categorization? Yes, they will.

Women prefer more informal language. By getting rid of the techno-speak on your site and speaking in plain English, will men benefit as well? Yes, we know, you're rumbling a bit here. "But guys like that technical stuff. It makes them feel that the company knows what they're talking about." There are still places where the "technical stuff" should be included: spec sheets, product detail pages, case studies, etc. If you're a phone company, you can still talk about your IPBX phone lines. But you're going to have to explain what that is. And that's going to benefit everyone.

When Designing For a Man *Can Be Good for a Woman*

There are actually some male attributes that you should consider when designing for women or both sexes.

Men tend to speak in shorter, more precise sentences. They get to the point quickly. Women can meander around with longer, more conversational sentence structure. In the case of the Internet, the man's preference actually works much better. Shorter sentences with more simple structure and clear points work extremely well for this written medium.

Another case where a man's preference can create a better experience for all parties is in color. Color blindness is a common occurrence for men. They can't tell the difference between certain colors. You must take this into consideration in many areas, especially product colors. You must be clear about your colors. Esoteric names like "Sierra Mountain" or "Sunset" are problematic. Make sure that for colors, you try to include a name that lets the visitor know what the base color is—"Sunset Red" or "Sierra Mountain Green," for example. If you can't put it in the color name, put it in the product description. With different browsers and screen resolutions, it's very tough to control colors over the web. Is that navy blue or black? Tell them in the copy. Give your visitors as many clues as you can about the actual color.

Women Only

If you decide to create a women's only area or section, make sure there's a good reason for separating them out. If you're creating an OB-GYN wing at your local hospital, no man is going to argue with you or feel left out (he'll probably thank you for not making him go into that uncomfortable place). If you create a "women's" section of your store, sell products that are for women only. If you have "Do It Herself" clinics, also make sure you offer regular clinics that address men's home improvement issues (Home Depot offers both).

Improving the Experience for All

How can you improve the experience women have in your store or on your website? Sales people ready to answer your questions; wider aisles; better lighting; product displays that show how a product is actually used; websites that provide clear navigation and calls to action; providing resources for choosing a plumber; and clear explanations of technical terms. All of these features will improve the experience women have at your store or site, but chances are very good it will also improve the experience men have as well.

Conclusion

It's easy to get super focused on exciting ways to market to women, but beware the trap of thinking that marketing to women means excluding men. By creating strong brand awareness through development of personas and speaking the language of the right brain, you will attract a parade of female customers *and* you'll discover an entire regiment of men following directly behind. Immerse yourself in, then implement the techniques presented in this book. You'll become a better businessperson. Your company will become a better company. And oh, yes . . . you'll also see more profit than you could have ever imagined. Next up, some ideas on how to get started.

22

Putting Your Plan into Action

A sailor meets a pirate in a bar, and they take turns telling about their adventures on the high seas. The sailor notices the pirate has a peg leg, a hook for a hand, and a patch over his eye.

The sailor says, "Say, I see you have a peg leg."

"Arrgh . . . aye, matey," the pirate replies. "'Twas in a storm at sea, and was swept overboard into a school of sharks. As the men pulled me out, a shark bit me leg clean off."

"Wow!" said the sailor. "And I see you have a hook."

"Aye," replied the pirate. "We had boarded an enemy ship and were battlin' the other sailors with swords. A large wave knocked me off balance and the enemy cut me hand clean off."

"Incredible!" said the sailor. "And how did you get that eye patch?"

"A seagull pooped in me eye," replied the pirate.

"You lost your eye to seagull poop?" the sailor asked incredulously.

"Arrgh . . . no, matey," said the pirate. "'Twas me first day with the hook."

With this book, our goal has been to present some powerful techniques for marketing to women that, if done correctly, will have a very large impact on your bottom line. On their own, each technique produces more knowledge about women as consumers than you could have discovered on your own. Combined, they are a profit-bearing powerhouse.

In other words, we've given you a very large hook to work with. But if you're not careful and start swinging it around without knowing what you're doing, you'll put an eye out.

Give yourself enough time to absorb everything we've covered in this book. But more important, make sure whatever conclusions you come to work for your individual business. When it comes to marketing to women, one size does not fit all.

The Rah-Rahs and the Lock 'n' Loads

MICHELE: If I were Native American, my tribal name would be Bucket of Cold Water.

As Holly and I spend more and more time on the speaking circuit, we find that presenters basically fall into two groups, the Rah-Rahs and the Lock 'n' Loads. The Rah-Rahs are those well-oiled showmen whose motivation is to get you fired up about a topic of choice, draw you into their momentary sphere of influence, and convince you that all your challenges will be solved with their simple fix. You're charged up when you leave the room, but it isn't long before real life taps you on the shoulder, reminding you of the overflowing to-do list, the phone calls to return and everyday business that needs your attention. You might feel like the star quarterback for a couple of days, but soon it's back to life as the water boy.

Holly and I like to think of ourselves as more the Lock 'n' Load type. The Lock 'n' Loads are there to give it to you straight. They know the importance of a show, but don't let it get in the way of the knowledge they want to impart. They give you a thrill, the gift of a new perspective, and information you can use. Then they hit you with a splash of cold water. They remind you that real life will be waiting in the lobby when the session is finished. This time, as you leave the room, you're saying, "I can do this. Well, maybe not all of it right away. But I can take one thing and apply it to my business . . . and it will make a difference."

When speaking to audiences across the country about marketing to women, we focus on sharing a number of important key points that businesses need to understand in order to create an effective marketing strategy. Depending on the time allotted, we present a variety of steps that businesses can take to reach female consumers; the exercises that accompany each step are not only fun, they're eye-opening for the participants. Suddenly, it's clear why previous marketing plans haven't been more effective and, in some cases, why their staff isn't performing up to expectations. Dividing the topic of marketing to women into bite-size pieces immediately reduces its overwhelming nature—lightbulbs go on and people get genuinely fired up.

Then the bucket of cold water.

In an attempt to bring them back to earth, we end each seminar with a mini lecture that no Rah-Rah we know would ever dare give. "What we've just covered," we say, "is exciting and offers great promise. You're seeing new ways to connect with female consumers and you're very motivated right now. You can choose any one of the steps we've worked on today and you'll see a definite increase in profitability."

"But it won't be easy. You're up against two big barriers. One, change isn't easy. It's hard to radically change the way you do business and the way you market your products. Two, unconscious bias is always at play. Men and women all have biases we aren't aware of. We all stereotype. We all buy into outdated and sometimes false ideas of who women really are and what they really want. You will get resistance. Trust us. It always happens. Be ready to have hard-core research and statistics to back up your ideas."

How to Get Started

If we had to prioritize how to effectively understand and implement the marketing to women platform, here's what we would suggest:

Acknowledge women as the mainstream consumers of today . . . and tomorrow. You already know she controls more than eighty cents of every dollar spent in the United States. But the real reason marketing to women is here to stay is the "perfect storm" convergence of purchasing power and mass adoption of the Internet. Women are saying, "I want consumer equality; treat me as an individual with individual needs."

Understand the foundation of gender difference in marketing. By recognizing the unique qualities each gender has when it comes to brain wiring, you've acquired the knowledge that women tap into the right brain of emotion, experience, and intuition much more quickly than men do. Combined with the "nurture" elements of society, the environment, and communication styles, you begin to see that marketing to women requires an entirely different language than has been spoken by many generations of traditional marketers.

Throw stereotypes out the window . . . immediately. There really is no such thing as a Soccer Mom. Today's society is so different from the way it was twenty years ago. We're dealing with different mind-sets, different roles, with elements like age and values that are wildly varied. Stereotypes have a negative connotation for both the consumer and the advertiser. It's much more difficult to market to stereotypes, especially when you don't understand them and, in some cases, don't even like them. Have the courage to go beyond the norm and open the window to a new view on marketing to women.

Start thinking of your consumers as women with individual needs. Spend time with Maslow's hierarchy of needs and determine which level of need your business currently serves. Do this, and your message will automatically resonate with customers needing you most. Once you have this covered, kick it up a notch for superbrand awareness and deliver one step higher. Remember BMW, Starbucks, and Apple—they are cult brands because they are focused on serving a higher level of need than their competitors.

Create a set of personas that represent the different needs of female consumers. By talking to everyone you may not be truly connecting with anyone. Find out what your customers have in common, but also how they are different. Accommodate their differing needs, motivations, questions, and objections. Create messages that resonate with each one of your personas. Connect with her not as a "niche group" but as an individual.

Place the personas in buying scenarios to create persuasive pathways so that both you and your customers can meet your goals. Where is she experiencing problems with your sales process? What are the points at which she hits a dead end, or experiences a disconnect in the customer experience? Take the time to actually plan scenarios so you can meet all her needs and answer her questions at the point at which she is asking them. Plan for every micro action along the way with clear next steps to create persuasive momentum. Planning scenarios will enable you not only to satisfy your customers but delight them, too.

Increase your depth of knowledge with research that goes beyond the "*what*" to the "*why*." Stop relying on traditional methods of research. If it hasn't given you reliable insight in the past, why keep doing it? Start talking to real women about their lives. Form conversation groups for friends to tell you about their lives, dreams, and worries. Use online surveys and blogs to connect with women in their homes, where they feel most comfortable (and anonymous). Utilize ideas like photo contests and in-home visits to see how people really live and use your product or service.

Give your message a voice that's real, authentic, and relevant to more than one woman. Stop using marketing-speak and techno-talk, and start speaking from your heart. Find your core value and focus everything in your business around it. It's not enough to speak in a strong marketing language; you have to know how to relate your core message to the different dialects of the four buying modes. If you can persuade a woman to do business with you no matter what buying mode she's in, you'll win every time.

Everything is marketing. Everything is marketing. Everything is marketing. Each and every touch point of your business contains an element of marketing, from answering the phone, to the lighting in your store, to the cleanliness of your bathrooms. Pin a copy of the Wheel of Persuasion on the wall over your desk. Do you have all the elements covered? And do you have them covered for each buying mode? Who are the leaders within your staff? You can't do it all yourself; delegation is key to a highly successful marketing strategy.

Keep your eye on the future of marketing and technology. Changes in the way people are utilizing technology and connecting with one another are happening at warp speed. Daily improvements in cell phones, computers, iPods, and other forms of technology are adding up to a societal revolution. Now is the time to keep your finger on the pulse of what's happening and how it will affect your business . . . *because it will.* Traditional advertising like the Yellow Pages aren't enough. Make sure you tap into the incredible power of the Internet. You must have an Internet presence and it must be female-friendly. It's the era of extreme customer empowerment, and you'd better be ready to give them what they want when they want it.

Conclusion

No one ever said marketing to women was easy. It requires total concentration on the female consumer as a wise and wonderful individual, with a life that looks more like a colorful tapestry than a one-dimensional description on a sheet of paper. Your devotion to serving her needs, in a language she understands and a buying mode that resonates with her, will be challenging but worth every bit of work you put into it.

Try the steps we've outlined above in the prioritized order if you can. But before attempting any one of these steps, be sure to ask yourself two questions:

1. **Do we have the skill?**

   Do we have the resources—money, time, energy, personnel—to make this one step happen? If we don't, are we willing to devote more resources or do more work to make it happen? Is it the most appropriate step for us right now?

2. **Do we have the will?**

   If we decide to try it, do we have the endurance to go the long haul and see this through to its end? If things don't work out as we'd hoped, do we have the guts and flexibility to adjust to the situation, or will we cave in?

Can you answer "yes" to both questions? If not, refocus before moving forward. But don't give up. Just keep tossing around ideas until you have one you can actually *accomplish*. Then grab that ball and run like heck with it.

We want this book to fire you up, but we also want you to always ask yourself both of these questions to keep your feet on the ground. The success of every marketing idea you choose to implement, especially when it comes to marketing to women, depends on your level of commitment and follow-through. It's only when you can take action on a marketing plan, even when real life is tapping you on the shoulder, that you'll experience the triumph you've envisioned.

Good luck. We can't wait to hear about your success!

Final Thoughts—*Holly*

Like it or not, advertising affects us, often more deeply than we realize. I believe one of the reasons why people are increasingly filtering out ads, whether electronically or emotionally, is to protect themselves. We literally want to protect and shield ourselves from these messages. I believe this is true for both sexes, but I think it's especially true for women.

Yeah, I know, I study advertising for a living, so I may be extra sensitive to it. One of my best friends from Richmond always chides me with her rich southern accent "Darlin' . . . you're just so SENsitive." But the images of women portrayed in advertising DO affect us.

What happens when day in and day out you don't see images of yourself, your situation, your emotions, your pains, your values, your life? I can't speak for everyone, but it makes me feel more isolated. When you don't see yourself reflected in the world around you, it is all too easy to ask, "What's wrong with me?"

Take an example of holiday advertising. So many people feel alone, isolated, and sad around the holidays. There's just something about the holidays that tends to stir up emotions in us. Yet look at holiday ads. They are full of laughing people, happy children, family gatherings, romantic couples. Where are the ads that acknowledge the loneliness or sense of isolation many experience around the holidays?

One of my strongest holiday memories was when my family came down to share Thanksgiving with me in Virginia. My sister flew in from Los Angeles where she and her husband had just decided to get a divorce. When I asked her what she wanted to do for the holiday weekend, she replied, "Sit on the floor in the bathroom and drink tequila."

Not wanting to disappoint, I lighted candles all through my tiny upstairs bathroom, sneaked in a bottle of Patron and two shot glasses, and stole my sister away from the crowd and into the bathroom to shoot tequila. She sat on the commode, I sat on the bathtub rim, and we saluted family and cursed men and poured Patron down our throats. I actually don't think I've ever felt closer to my sister than at that time.

So now, every Thanksgiving we grab a bottle of tequila and some shot glasses, and disappear into a bathroom. We've even started inviting a very precious few to join us in this tradition. If other guests notice we're missing, a knowing relative will say, "They're probably in the bathroom shooting tequila." This usually garners the response "*No—where are they, really?*" At which point the exasperated relative will reply again, "Really—they're sitting on the toilet going a few rounds with Jose Cuervo. Give 'em a few minutes. They'll be back."

Where are the holiday commercials that reflect the kind of pain my sister was feeling that Thanksgiving? It doesn't have to be a negative commercial. Surely some advertiser could create a touching story of two sisters sneaking away from the holiday crowd and going into the bathroom with a bottle of the client's spirits and two glasses to curse their lives but count their blessings in each other.

You're acknowledging that people have a tough time during the holidays, but it's still an uplifting moment of two sisters bonding.

Faced with a sea of holiday commercials that show big parties, happy couples, and boisterous, laughter-filled gatherings, for the woman who feels lost and little alone, I bet this commercial would be a welcome change.

So my challenge to you is to be courageous, have some guts, dare to be different. It won't be easy, believe me; people will fight you on it. But in this day and age, when so many companies still don't get it, if you create genuine messages that reflect who she really is, she WILL notice you.

If you've really taken the time to understand your customers, if you've really tapped into a deeply felt truth, portray that in your advertising. Not only will you win her business; you'll win her loyalty, as a customer and as a person.

I can't wait to see what you come up with.

Final Thoughts—*Michele*

Holly said I should drink a bottle of wine and share my thoughts on Dove's Campaign for Real Beauty.

Actually, she said drink a *glass,* but some topics are worthy of a whole damned case. And Dove is the perfect example of why I'm so passionate about marketing to women.

You see, Dove's success touches the very essence of my passion for great works of art. And that's hard to talk about, because every masterpiece, be it a symphony, a book, a film, or a scientific theory, requires the interpreter to open up and reconnect with a very vulnerable, sometimes painful space hidden within herself.

Not all artists are willing to take such a risk; they work hard to keep their public in a comfort zone. But others are driven to push through the clutter with a new message that sometimes shocks, sometimes angers, sometimes resonates. It is a message so salient, it reverberates around the globe.

Amazingly, Dove has taken that artistic risk, and in doing so, it is creating a masterpiece of marketing.

The first time you spot Dove's billboard featuring real women with real bodies in their undies, you silently applaud the effort. Then you start reading articles about these ads and go to the Dove website for more information. You're stunned to find that an entire community of women has sprouted up out of nowhere. There are articles, surveys, and videos of everyday women talking about what "real beauty" is, and open discussion about one of the most private, hush-hush topics among women of all ages: poor body image. Like me, you knew you weren't alone each time you asked the question, "What's wrong with me?" But you didn't have the guts to talk about it openly. Not until Dove came along and started the conversation for you.

It would have been easy for Dove to stop after a onetime, flash-in-the-pan successful ad campaign. But they just keep peeling back the layers. When watching a man rendered nearly speechless with love in trying to describe his ordinary wife's beauty in an ad for Energy Glow lotion, husbands turn to their wives and say,

"That's how I feel about you." Men and women alike are brought to tears every time I show the True Colors television ad, which took on the body issues of young girls by launching Dove's Self-Esteem Fund. And as I sit here writing these final words, a new article in *Ad Age* says Dove's latest venture, a seventy-five-second film illustrating how the cosmetics industry distorts an ordinary woman into a supermodel, with lighting, makeup, and Photoshop, has been viewed nearly two million times on YouTube and is getting better ROI than a Super Bowl ad.

In one fell swoop, Dove walked up to its own industry and smacked it across the face for years of distortion, lies, and manipulation. With that one slap, every woman in America was given permission to exhale, including me. I was almost relieved to reveal the image of myself I've carried around inside all these years, that of a ten-year-old girl with tortoise shell glasses, a shag haircut, and crooked teeth who always thought she was fat.

Dove took the risk of climbing into the right brains of females and pressed that very delicate area of emotional experience, bringing up painful memories and feelings about body image. They set the stage, then let the message speak for itself, thereby allowing women to do the talking, cheering, and healing. And, in the end, they built a brand loyalty so strong, it will take an atomic bomb to destroy it.

How much grief has Dove gotten over this campaign, given they are a company that manufactures beauty products? Plenty, judging from critiques by ad execs and comments on my blog. But as with any campaign that goes out on a limb, grief's a given. The fact that folks are so riled up over this (not to mention the tremendous profit margin) is evidence it's hitting the mark.

When a company like Dove gets it so right and does everything it can to deliver an authentic, powerful message based on individual women's needs and experiences, it fills my heart as much as when I hear a triumphant symphony, watch a timeless film, or read great literature. I see the potential for businesses to grow beyond their wildest dreams simply by speaking a language that women understand, and it makes me want to sing.

More than anything, it gives me hope. Hope that more companies will start speaking as clearly and honestly as Dove. And hope that business owners and executives will start taking some risks in speaking to women in a way that not only creates profit, but changes the very mirror they peer into when trying to connect through advertising.

I have hope for this marketing world of ours. I have hope for you. Now go make a masterpiece.